THE MUSIC BOOK

Eunice Boardman
Professor of Music Education
University of Wisconsin
Madison, Wisconsin

Barbara Andress
Professor of Music Education
Arizona State University
Tempe, Arizona

Special Consultants

Beth Landis
Former Director of Music Education
City Schools
Riverside, California

Betty Welsbacher
Director of Special Music Education
Wichita State University
Wichita, Kansas

Consultants

Martha Mahoney
Elementary Music Department Head
Elementary Schools
Milford, Connecticut

Donald Regier
Supervisor of Vocal Music
Secondary Schools
Baltimore County, Maryland

Keith Thompson
Associate Professor, Music Education
Pennsylvania State University
University Park, Pennsylvania

Nelmatilda Woodard
Director, Bureau of Music Education
Board of Education
City of Chicago

Holt, Rinehart and Winston, Publishers
New York, Toronto, London, Sydney

Portions of this book previously published as EXPLORING MUSIC ♩♩♩
Copyright © 1975, 1971, 1966 by Holt, Rinehart and Winston, Publishers

Copyright © 1981 by Holt, Rinehart and Winston, Publishers
All rights reserved
Printed in the United States of America
ISBN: 0-03-042171-3
12345 071 9876543

ACKNOWLEDGMENTS

Grateful acknowledgment is given to the following authors and publishers:

American Folklore, Inc., for "Old Hen," from 1939 *Journal of American Folklore.* Used by permission.

M. Baron Company for "Tinga Layo." Copyright 1943 by M. Baron Company. Used by permission.

Berandal Music Company for "The Little Prince," French Songs, translated by Alan Mills, from *Whales and Nightingales,* Terry-Shind Churchbey. Used by permission.

Blackwood Music, Inc., for "Cloud Song," by Joseph Byrd and Dorothy Moskowitz. Copyright © 1968 by Blackwood Music, Inc. International Copyright Secured. All Rights Reserved. Used by permission.

The Bodley Head for "I've a Fine Bonny Castle," from *The Children's Song Book* by Elizabeth Poston, published by The Bodley Head. Used by permission.

Walt Disney Music Company for "The Unbirthday Song." Words and music by Mack David, Al Hoffman, and Jerry Livingston. Copyright 1948 by Walt Disney Music Company. For "Siamese Cat Song." Words and music by Peggy Lee and Sonny Burke. Copyright 1953 by Walt Disney Music Company. Used by permission.

Doubleday & Co., Inc., for "Mice" by Rose Fyleman. From *Favorite Poems Old and New,* edited by Helen Ferris. Used by permission.

European American Music for "Let's Build a Town," by Paul Hindemith.

Frank Music Corp., for "The Ugly Duckling," by Frank Loesser. Copyright 1951, 1952 by Frank Music Corp. International Copyright Secured. All Rights Reserved. Used by permission.

Gordon Press for "Rain Chant," from the *Indian's Book,* translated by Natalie Curtis Burlin. Used by permission.

Gloria Hamm for "Willowbee." Used by permission.

Charles Haywood for "The Gazelle," from *Folk Songs of the World.* Used by permission.

Charles Hansen Music Company for "Hill and Gully Rider," from Charles Hansen Educational Music and Books. Copyright © 1976. For "At a Georgia Camp Meeting," by Kerry Mills from the *Jumbo Magic Song Book.* Copyright © 1975 by Shattinger-International Music Corporation. Used by permission.

Harper & Row, Publishers, Inc., for "The Snake," from *In The Middle of the Trees* by Karla Kuskin. Copyright © 1958 by Karla Kuskin. Used by permission.

Holt, Rinehart and Winston of Canada Limited for "Hallowe'en," music by John Wood for "Come Boating with Me," words by Lansing Macdowell from *Songtime 4* by Vera Russel, *et al.* Copyright © 1963 by Holt, Rinehart and Winston of Canada, Limited, Publishers, Toronto. Used by permission.

Little, Brown & Company for "Between Birthdays," from *Verses from 1929 On* by Ogden Nash. Copyright © 1961, 1962 by Ogden Nash. Used by permission.

Ludlow Music, Inc., for "Way Down Yonder in the Brickyard." New words and new music adaptation by Bessie Jones. Collected and edited by Alan Lomax. TRO-Copyright © 1972 Ludlow Music, Inc. For "Good-By, Old Paint." Collected, adapted, and arranged by John A. Lomax and Alan Lomax. TRO-Copyright © 1934 and renewed © 1962 Ludlow Music, Inc. For "Po' Lil' Jesus." Collected, adapted, and arranged by John A. Lomax and Alan Lomax. TRO-Copyright 1947 and renewed © 1975 Ludlow Music, Inc. For "I'm Going Away to See Aunt Dinah." New words and new music arrangement by Bessie Jones and Alan Lomax. TRO-Copyright © 1972 and renewed © 1977 Ludlow Music, Inc. Used by permission.

McClelland Stewart Ltd., for "Why, Sir." (Ball-bouncing rhyme.) Used by permission.

New Directions Corporation for "The Sower," from *Anthology of Contemporary Latin-American Poetry,* edited by Dudley Pitts. Copyright 1942 by New Directions Publishing Corporation. Used by permission.

Peter Paul Press for So-in, Basho and Taigai. Japanese Haiki. Used by permission.

Alfred A. Knopf, Inc., for "Dream Dust," from *The Panther and the Lash: Poems of Our Times,* by Langston Hughes. Copyright 1947 by Langston Hughes. Used by permission.

CONTENTS

Unit I   MUSIC TO EXPLORE   1

The First Quarter   1

The Second Quarter   22

The Third Quarter   40

The Fourth Quarter   62

Unit II   MORE MUSIC TO EXPLORE   84

Perform by Singing and Playing   85

Describe Music   112

Create Music   124

Special Times   136

MUSIC
TO EXPLORE

The First Quarter

CHILDREN

Words and Music by Barbara Andress

Snap your fingers while you sing.

1. and 4. Chil-dren, *(echo)* chil-dren, *(echo)*

Let's all tra-vel down the glo-ry road. *(echo)*

2. Two by two, *(echo)*
   Four by four, *(echo)*
   Children on the glory road by the score. *(echo)*

3. Walking on the flat land, *(echo)*
   Walking o'er the fields, *(echo)*
   Walking up the mountain with the glory shield. *(echo)*

How will you travel down the glory road?

high?

Can you move

Flip to the side.

1

LONG JOHN

Afro-American Folk Song

Listen to the melody. When does it go up? down?
Use your hand to show how the melody moves.

With his shiny blade,
Got it in his hand,
Gonna chop out the live oaks
That are in this land.
He's Long John,
He's long gone,
He's gone, gone,
Like a turkey in the corn,
With his long clothes on.
He's Long John,
He's long gone,
He's gone.

Move Around

Step short sounds.
Clap longer sounds.

STEP

CLAP

One person plays **bongo drums.**

HIGH

LOW

Change Around

Step longer sounds. STEP

Clap short sounds. CLAP

Another person plays a rhythm pattern on bells.

CHANGE AROUND without stopping when you hear . . .

1   2   read · y CHANGE!

Choose one of these ideas. Use it to accompany "Long John."

LET'S BUILD A TOWN

by Paul Hindemith

Follow the words. Which parts will sound the same?
Where will the melody move down by steps?
Where will it skip back and forth?

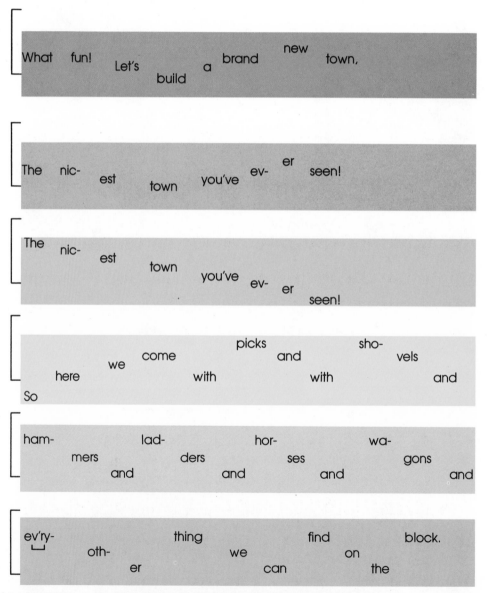

What fun! Let's build a brand new town,
The nic- est town you've ev- er seen!
The nic- est town you've ev- er seen!
So here we come with picks and with sho- vels and
ham- mers and lad- ders and hor- ses and wa- gons and
ev'ry- oth- er thing we can find on the block.

What fun! Let's build a brand new town,

The nic- est town you've ev- er seen.

Perform "Sounds of Builders." Begin with an accompaniment.

Start with the shortest sound.

Add a steady beat

and longer sounds.

One performer should play the rhythm of the melody
"Let's Build a Town." Use wood instruments.

THE
STEEL
FOUNDRY

from *Symphony of Machines*

by Alexander Mossolov

What sounds of rhythm would you hear in a factory?
What would make long sounds? short sounds?
Would any of the sounds be repeated like a steady beat?

Listen to the recording. In this music, a composer expresses
his idea of how a machine sounds.

Can you make a machine by moving to the music?
Use five people. Begin by entering one part at a time.
Will your motions be exactly the same? the opposite? different?
Will you be pistons? levers? chains? wheels? What else?

Body Presses and Assembly of Automobile Chassis (South Wall), Detail,
Diego Rivera (1886-1957, Mexico) Frescoes.
From the collection of The Detroit Institute of Arts. Gift of Edsel Ford.

TELL US GENTLEMEN

French Folk Song

1. Tell us gen - tle - men, Tell us all that you can do.
2. Tell us gen - tle - men, Tell us all that you can do.

Tell us gen - tle - men, can you play the big trom - bone?
Tell us gen - tle - men, can you play the tim - pa - ni?

Verses accumulate

Trom - bo trom - bo trom - bone!
Tim - po tim - po tim - po!

Tell us, oh, can you play the big trom - bone?
Tell us, oh, can you play the tim - pa - ni?

3. Tell us gentlemen . . .
Can you play the trumpet?
Trump-o, trump-o, trump-o.

4. Tell us gentlemen . . .
Can you play the violin?
Vi-o, vi-o, vi-o.

5. Tell us gentlemen . . .
Can you play the clarinet?
Clar-i, clar-i, net-o.

6. Tell us gentlemen . . .
Can you play the silver flute?
Flut-o, flut-o, flut-o.

RUSSIAN SAILORS' DANCE
from *The Red Poppy*

by Reinhold Glière

Listen to the melody. It is played by different instruments.
You will hear the melody twelve times.

Introduction

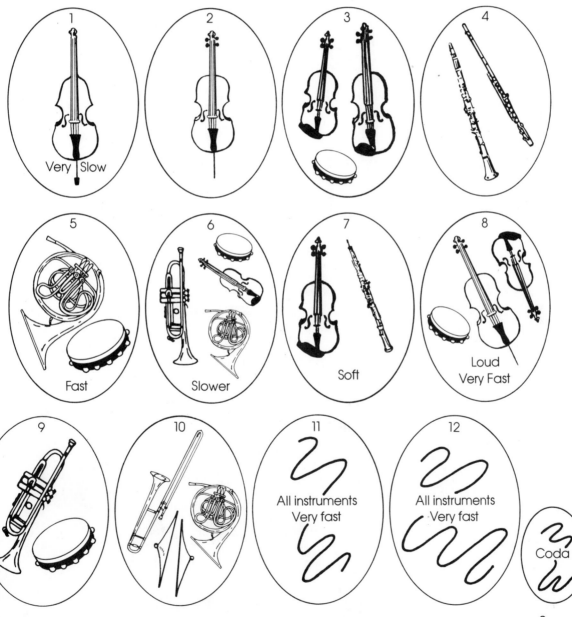

I'VE A FINE BONNY CASTLE

Traditional

Most of this song moves with short sounds.

When will it move with a longer sound?

Someone tap the short sounds.
Everyone chant the words.

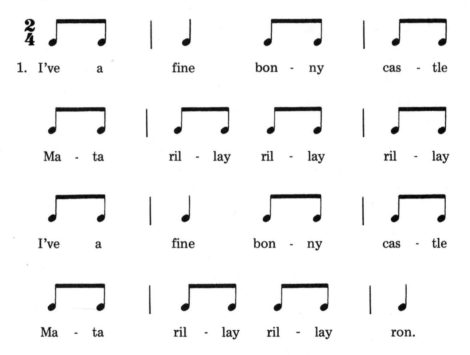

1. I've a fine bon - ny cas - tle
   Ma - ta ril - lay ril - lay ril - lay
   I've a fine bon - ny cas - tle
   Ma - ta ril - lay ril - lay ron.

2. May I come to your castle?
   Mata rillay rillay rillay.
   May I come to your castle?
   Mata rillay rillay ron.
3. Yes, do come to my castle. . . .
4. But you've locked up your castle. . . .
5. Find the key of my castle. . . .
6. Here's the key of your castle. . . .

Listen to the melody.
Can you draw its picture?
Will it begin like this?
Or like this?

MINUET

from *Sinfonia No. 1 in G Major*

by Domenico Scarlatti

1. Put your finger on line "1" and move it slowly as you listen.
2. The call numbers will tell you when to begin each new line.
3. Listen again. This time, draw an imaginary line to show how each melody ends.

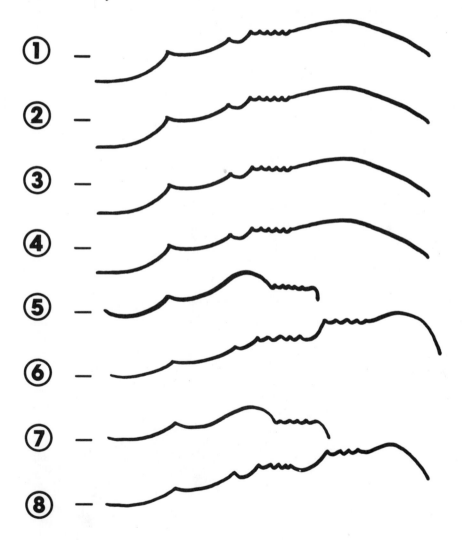

THE SIAMESE CAT SONG

from *Lady and the Tramp*

Words and Music by Peggy Lee
and Sonny Burke

Read the rhythm of this song.
It begins with short sounds.
When does it change
to a longer sound?
When will you be silent?

C   **C**

1. We are Si - a - mee - iz if you plee - iz,

C   **G7**

We are Si - a - mee - iz if you don't please.

G7   **G7**

We are for - mer res - i - dents of Si - am.

G7   **C**

There is no fin - er cat than I am.

2. We are Siamese with very dainty claws.
    Please observing paws containing dainty claws.
    Now we lookin' over our new domicile,
    If we like we stay for maybe quite awhile.

3. Who is that who's living in that wire house?
    It must be a bird because it's not a mouse.
    If we sneakin' up upon it carefully,
    There will be some bird for you and some for me.

4. Do you seeing that thing swimmin' 'round and 'round?
    Maybe we could reaching in and make it drown.
    If we sneakin' up upon it carefully,
    There will be a head for you, a tail for me.

Play an accompaniment made up of short sounds.

WOOD BLOCK

Play an introduction and a coda.

XYLOPHONE

CLOUD SONG

Words by Dorothy Moskowitz   Music by Joseph Byrd

How do you think cloud music should sound? Listen.
Did it sound the way you thought it would?

How sweet to be a___ cloud___ float-ing in the___ blue___ it makes him ve-ry___ proud___ to be a lit-tle cloud.___ How sweet to be___ a___ cloud___ float-ing in___ the___ blue.___

Will you sing this song the same way you sang "The Siamese

Cat Song"? ~~~~~~ *legato?* or ·····•·····•····· *staccato?*

ANITRA'S DANCE
from *Peer Gynt Suite*

by Edvard Grieg

This music uses both *staccato* and *legato* sounds.
Here is a picture of the music.
Can you follow it as you listen?

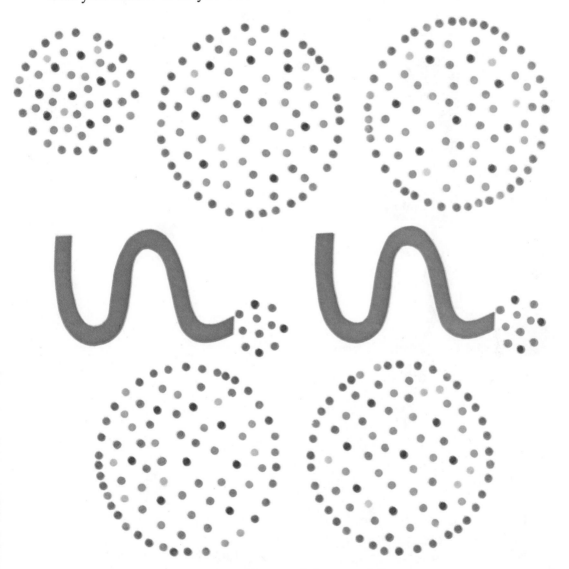

Can you make your own picture of the music?
Listen again. Do you hear other *legato* or *staccato* sounds
that you could draw?

Whole—Part: A Dance

Count aloud:

1   2   3   4   5   6   7   8   9   10   11   12   13   14   15   16

Create a whole dance using sixteen counts, or beats.

Can you break your whole dance into two parts?
How many beats will be in each part?
How will you let your audience know when the first part ends?

Add the ideas of other dancers to yours.
Create a whole dance with many parts.

A Poem

WHY, SIR?

Traditional

Are you coming out, sir?
No, sir. Why, sir?
Because I've got a cold, sir.
Where'd you get the cold, sir?
At the North Pole, sir.
What were you doing there, sir?
Catching polar bears, sir.
How many did you catch, sir?
One, sir, two, sir, three, sir,
That's enough for me, sir.

Read the whole poem.
How many parts are in this poem?
How do you know when each part ends?

The Snail, 1953 Henri Matisse
(1869-1954, France).
Gouache on cut-and-
pasted paper.
The Tate Gallery, London.
Permission S.P.A.D.E.M. 1974 by
French Reproduction Rights, Inc.

WHO'S THAT YONDER?

Spiritual

Read the poem.
How many parts does it have?
How do you know?

Look at the music.
How many parts does it have?
What do you see that helps you decide?

Poem:
Who's that yonder dressed in red?
Must be the children that Moses led.
Who's that yonder dressed in white?
Must be the children of the Israelite.

FOUR IN A BOAT

Appalachian Mountain Song

Shorter parts of songs are called **phrases.**

You can sense the end of a phrase because the music seems to come to rest.

How many phrases do you sense in this song?

TAMBOURIN

from *Danses d'Acante et Cephise*

by Jean-Phillippe Rameau

Listen to the music.
Follow the boy's or the girl's dance movements.
Can you tell when they pause to greet each other? Can you tell
when they come to a stop at the end of a phrase?
How many times could they repeat this pattern?

Plan your own dance to show the phrases.
Move with the same feeling.
When will you want to move in different directions?

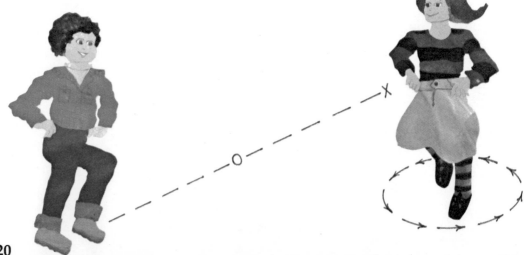

HOW DO YOU MEASURE UP? (1)

Can you
    tap the shortest sounds?
    clap the steady beat?
    perform long and short sounds at the same time?
    hear melodies that go up, down, stay the same?
    find musical phrases?
    perform *staccato* and *legato* sounds?
    sing songs expressively?

MORNING SONG

Words by Jane Rolfe Randolph   American Folk Hymn

Expressively

1. Dawn is like a ___ gate that o - pens

On a mead - ow ___ wide and fair.

Through the o - pen gate I hur - ry;

Gold - en light ___ is ___ ev - ery - where.

The Second Quarter

LONE STAR TRAIL

American Cowboy Song

Look at the picture.
What do you notice?

Follow the picture as you listen to the melody.
What do you hear?

1. I started on the trail on June twenty-third,
    I been punchin' Texas cattle on the Lone Star Trail;
    Refrain: Singin' Ki yi yippy, yippy yay, yippy yay!
    Singin' Ki yi yippy, yippy yay!

2. I get up in the morn before the daylight,
    And before I go to sleep the moon is shining bright.
    Refrain

3. It's bacon and it's beans almost every day,
    But I wouldn't mind a change if it was prairie hay.
    Refrain

The curved line kept coming back to the same place.
The melody kept coming back to the same pitch.
This is the **tonal center** of the melody.

DERRY DING DING DASON

English Round

Most melodies keep returning to one important pitch.
We call this pitch the **tonal center.**
Can you tell when the melody touches the tonal center in this
song?

1.
Der-ry ding ding da - son,   I   am John Ches - ton,

2.
We   wee - don, we   wo - don, We   wee - don, we   wo - don,

3.
Bim   boom,   bim   boom,   bim   boom,   bim   boom.

ALL THE LITTLE BABIES

American Folk Tune

Can you find a high and low tonal center?

COME BOATING WITH ME

Words by Lansing MacDowell

Italian Folk Song

The tonal center of a song is called "1."
Play and sing a major scale by starting and ending on the tonal center.

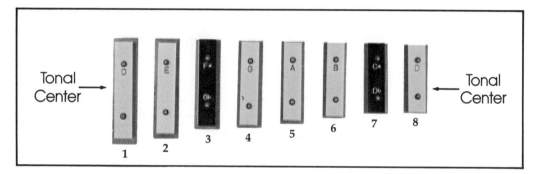

Tonal Center →

← Tonal Center

Read this song using the scale numbers.

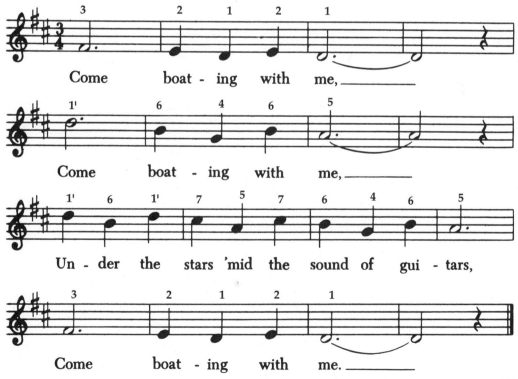

Come boat - ing with me, _____

Come boat - ing with me, _____

Un - der the stars 'mid the sound of gui - tars,

Come boat - ing with me. _____

I'M A NUT

Traditional

Tune up:

			5		
		3		3	
	1				1
	F				

Sing and play these four phrases.
What is the same about each? What is different?

Are the phrases in the right order to make a whole song?
How can you tell?
Put them in an order that sounds right to you.

Sing these words with the melody.

I'm an acorn small and round
Lying on the cold, cold ground.
People come and step on me;
That's why I'm so cracked, you see!

THE NOBLE DUKE OF YORK

American Folk Song

Can you decide by looking at this song which pitch is the tonal center?

1. The no - ble Duke of York,
2. And when they were up they were up,

He had ten thou - sand men;
And when they were down they were down,

He marched them up to the top of the hill,
And when they were caught in be - tween,

Then marched them down a - gain.
They were neith - er up nor down.

Rainstorm

Here are the sounds of:

wind))))))) rub palms together

small raindrops · · · · · · click tongue

big raindrops 🌢🌢🌢🌢🌢 pat knees

lightning ⚡⚡ clap hands twice

thunder ∿∿∿∿∿ stamp feet, becoming louder,
then softer

Perform the rainstorm.
Follow this score.

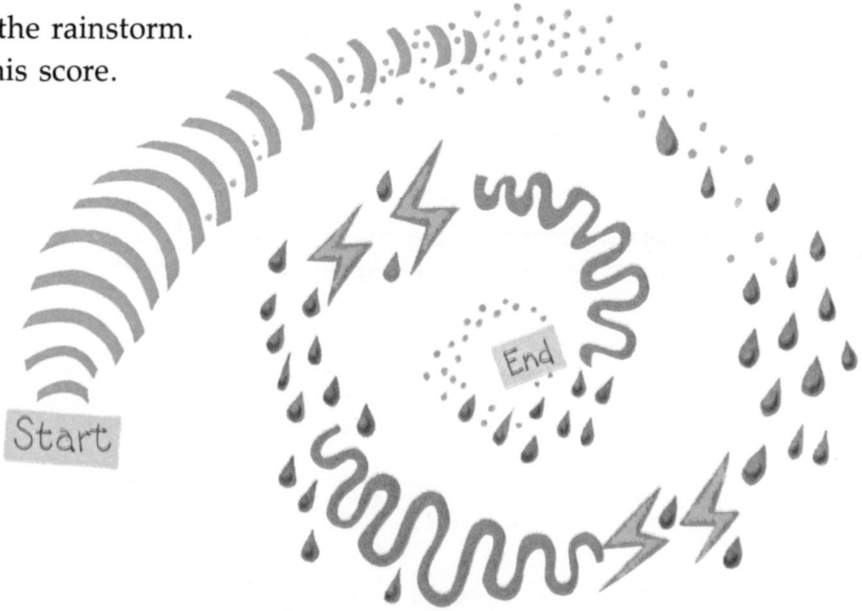

Start

End

When was your storm loudest? softest?
How did you perform to make it loud? soft?
Perform the storm on instruments.
How will you decide what instruments to use?

THIS HOUSE IS HAUNTED

American Folk Song

How can you use voices and instruments to help express
the ideas in this song?
Will you use sounds that

are loud?   are soft?   get louder?   get softer?

This house is haunt - ed, this house is haunt - ed,

It fair - ly makes my blood run cold. _____

This house is haunt - ed, this house is haunt - ed,

It fair - ly makes my blood run cold.

Sing "The Noble Duke of York" again.
Follow the signs that tell you to sing loud or soft.

Perform

Move . . .

alone

with others doing
the same thing

with others doing
different things
at the same time

Speak . . . Crossing it alone
in cold moonlight . . .
the brittle bridge
echoes my footsteps.
Taigi

alone

with others doing
the same thing

with others doing
different things
at the same time

Perform

alone	with others doing the same thing	with others doing different things at the same time

OLD TEXAS

Cowboy Song

1. I'm goin' to leave _____ old _ Tex - as now, _____
They've got no use _____ for the long- horn cow. _____

2. They've plowed and fenced my cattle range,
   And the people there are all so strange.
3. I'll take my horse, I'll take my rope,
   And hit the trail upon a lope.
4. Say adios to the Alamo,
   And turn my head toward Mexico.
5. I'll make my home on the wide wide range,
   For the people there are not so strange.
6. The hard hard ground shall be my bed,
   And my saddle seat shall hold my head.

When we perform different pitches at the same time we are singing and playing **in harmony.**

SARASPONDA

Dutch Spinning Song

Sa - ra- spon- da, Sa - ra- spon- da, Sa - ra- spon- da, Ret - set - set!

Sa - ra- spon - da, Sa - ra- spon- da, Sa - ra- spon - da, Ret - set - set!

Ah - do - ray - oh!   Ah - do - ray- boom - day - oh!

Ah - do - ray-boom-day, Ret-set - set!   A - say - pa - say- oh!

Add a part to make harmony.
Sing "Boom-da" on the tonal center.

Boom-da, boom-da, boom-da, boom-da.

DONKEYS AND CARROTS

Belgian Round

Many melodies have a tonal center.
The harmony strengthens the feeling of the tonal center.

Accompany this song using the **I chord.** It is built on the
tonal center.

I chord: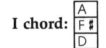

Don- keys love to munch on car - rots,

Car - rots don't love that at all!

Hee haw, Hee haw, Lis - ten to the sil - ly call.

Accompany Songs You Know

Accompany a song you know.
Use the **I** chord.

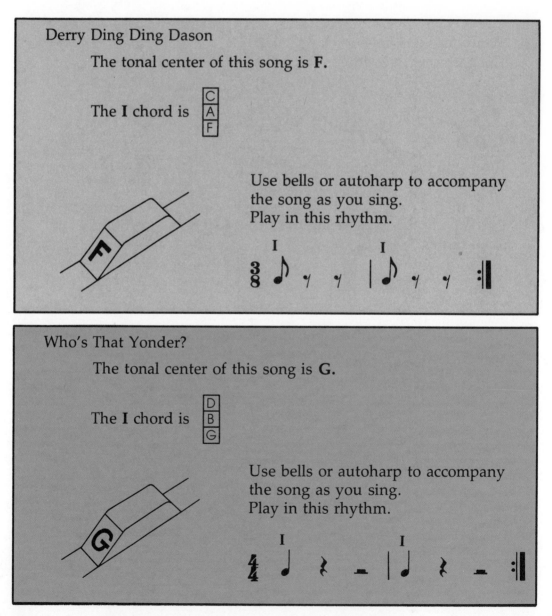

Derry Ding Ding Dason

The tonal center of this song is **F**.

The **I** chord is

C
A
F

Use bells or autoharp to accompany
the song as you sing.
Play in this rhythm.

Who's That Yonder?

The tonal center of this song is **G**.

The **I** chord is

D
B
G

Use bells or autoharp to accompany
the song as you sing.
Play in this rhythm.

I'M GOING AWAY TO SEE AUNT DINAH

Traditional

Melodies move around the tonal center.
Harmonies do, too.

Accompany the song using two chords: F and Dm

I'm going a - way, ___ see Aunt Di - nah,

I'm going a - way, ___ see my ___ Lord..

Bake them bis - cuits, bake 'em brown, See Aunt Di - nah, Turn.

___ them flap - jacks a - round and a - round See my ___ Lord..

New words and new music arrangement by Jessie Jones & Alan Lomax.
TRO-Copyright © 1972 renewed © 1977 Ludlow Music, Inc. Used by permission.

PICTURES AT AN EXHIBITION

by Modeste Moussorgsky

One day a composer named Moussorgsky visited an art show.
As he walked among the paintings, he decided to describe each
one with music. Visit the exhibition with Moussorgsky.
Listen to his music, then turn the paintings into living pictures.

Promenade

How does the composer feel as he **promenades** from one painting
to another? Proud? Afraid? Pleased? Show this in your movements.

Gnomes

What in the music will help you
decide how this painting will come
alive?

Tuilleries

Move as though you were
playing. Do you hear a
teasing pattern? Use the
same movement each time
you hear it.

Bydlo

Is the cart near or far away?
Is it heavy or light?
Are the people going to a picnic
or are they hard at work?
What musical ideas help you
decide?

Ballet of the Chicks
in Their Shells

How many chicks will there be?
Do they ever crack out
of their shells?
What do you hear that helps
you know?

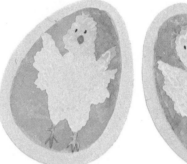

The Great Gate of Kiev

How many people will it take to make the great gate? As you
listen to the music, decide:
    when each person will move through the great gate.
    when the bell-ringers will pull the ropes.

You Visit
the Art Museum

Create music for one or both of these paintings.

*Person Throwing a
Stone at a Bird*, 1926
Joan Miro
Collection, The Museum
of Modern Art, New York

Play on Rocks, 1916
John Sloan
Hirshhorn Museum and
Sculpture Garden,
Smithsonian Institution
Joseph Martin/SCALA

Can you
hear the high and low tonal center of a song?
play or sing a song using scale numbers?
use musical symbols for loud, soft, getting louder,
and getting softer?
hear harmony?
perform a harmony part on an instrument?
identify instruments by sight and sound?

VESPER HYMN

Words by Thomas Moore

Music attributed to
Dmitri Bortniansky

Joyfully

Hark, the ves - per hymn is steal - ing
Near - er yet and near - er peal - ing,

O'er the wa - ters soft and clear.
Soft it breaks up - on the ear.

Ju - bi - la - te! Ju - bi - la - te!

Ju - bi - la - te! A - men.

39

The Third Quarter

THE GAZELLE

African Folk Song

Clap:

Leader

Look what the ga-zelle does.
Gbo- di man - gi we - re.

Group

Look what the ga-zelle does, do it, oh!
Gbo- di man - gi we - re, Gbo- di o.

Leader

Now she rolls her ears. __
Gbo- di wo ti turn. __

Group

Now she rolls her ears, __ do it, oh!
Gbo- di wo ti turn, __ Gbo- di o.

Leader

Now she shakes her tail.
Gbo- di gu a gu.

Group

Now she shakes her tail, do it, oh!
Gbo - di gu a gu, Gbo - di o.

Leader

Now she lies down to sleep.
Gbo - di sun - gun sen - de.

Group

Now she lies down to sleep, do it, oh!
Gbo - di sun - gun sen - de, Gbo - di o.

Leader

Now she jumps up.
Gbo - di gua - ri.

Group

Now she jumps up, do it, oh!
Gbo - di gua - ri, Gbo - di o.

Look at the music. What helps you know
when to group the beats in threes? in twos?

41

MY AUNT GRETE

Netherlands Folk Song

How will the beats be grouped in this song?

Look at the music. Is there an easy way to tell?

My Aunt Grete, vee - da vee - da vete, has a
And that tip, vee - da vee - da vip, has a

cat, vee - da vee - da vat, and that cat, vee-da vee-da
curl, vee - da vee - da vurl, and that curl, vee-da vee-da

vat, has a tail _____ And that tail, vee-da vee-da
curl, has a tail _____ And that tail, vee-da vee-da

vail, has a curl, vee - da vee - da vurl, and that
vail, has a cat, vee - da vee - da vat, and that

curl, vee - da vee - da vurl, has a tip. com - ma
cat, vee - da vee - da vat, has my aunt.

42

SANDY LAND

Words Adapted   American Singing Game

Play an accompaniment on the piano.
Play one pitch on the heavy beat at the beginning of each **measure.**
The pitches you will play are written above the staff.

1. Make my liv - ing in sand - y land,
2. Raise my ta - ters in sand - y land,
3. Keep on dig - ging in sand - y land,

Make my liv - ing in sand - y land,
Raise my ta - ters in sand - y land,
Keep on dig - ging in sand - y land,

Make my liv - ing in sand - y land,
Raise my ta - ters in sand - y land,
Keep on dig - ging in sand - y land,

La - dies, fare you well.

THE ANTS GO MARCHING

Traditional

March with the steady beat.
Step the **heavy** beat with your left foot.
Step the **light** beat with your right foot.

March while singing the song.

The ants go march-ing one by one, Hur-
ants go march-ing two by two, Hur-

rah! Hur-rah! The ants go march-ing
rah! Hur-rah! The ants go march-ing

one by one, hur-rah! Hur-rah! The
two by two, hur-rah! Hur-rah! The

ants go march-ing one by one. The
ants go march-ing two by two. The

last one stops to have some fun. The
last one stops to tie his shoe.

C7   F

ants   go   march - ing   round   and round   and

1.2.   F

3.   F

out   in   the   rain. 2. The
out   in   the   rain. 3. The   out   in   the   rain.

Whoop-De-Dah!

Change the accent. March with this chant.
Begin with the left foot on the accent.
When does the accent change to the right foot?

6/8   left   right

I left ___ I left ___ I left my shoe in Tim - buc - tu with

fif - ty holes and a buck-et of glue and I thought it was right, ___

___ right, ___ right for my blis - ter.   Whoop - de - dah!
(right - left-right)

Perform the chant over and over.
Begin loudly. Get softer each time except for the "Whoop-de-dah."
Follow these expression marks.

Chant	Whoop-de-dah
f	*ff*
mp	*ff*
p	*ff*
pp	*ff*

THE SOWER

by R. Olivares Figueroa
trans. by D. F.

On a white field,
black little seeds . . .
    Let it rain! rain!

"Sower, what do you sow?"
How the furrow sings!
    Let it rain! rain!

"I sow rainbows,
dawns and trumpets!"
    Let it rain! rain!

MICE

by Rose Fyleman

I think mice
Are rather nice.
    Their tails are long,
    Their faces small,
    They haven't any
    Chins at all.
    Their ears are pink,
    Their teeth are white,
    They run about
    The house at night.
    They nibble things
    They shouldn't touch
    And no one seems
    To like them much.
But I think mice
Are rather nice.

Read each poem.
Can you find ideas that are
    the same?   almost the same?   different?

Create a Composition

Use the guide sheets to make up your own music.

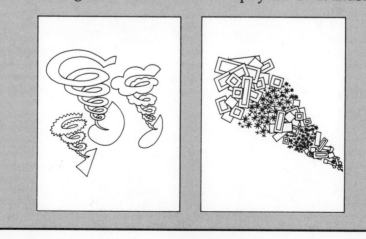

CIRCULAR FORMS

by Robert Delaunay

Look at the painting.
Can you find ideas that are the same? almost the same? different?

Circular Forms, 1912 Robert Delaunay (1885-1941, France). Oil on canvas.
The Solomon R. Guggenheim Museum Collection, New York.

RONDEAU

from *The Moor's Revenge*

by Henry Purcell

Listen to the music. Softly count to 24 as you listen.
Then begin again.

1 2 3 4 5 6 7 8 9 10 11 12 13 14 15 16 17 18 19 20 21 22 23 24

Each group of 24 counts in the music is one section of the composition.
How many sections did you count?
Listen again. Do some sections sound the **same?** How many are **different?**
Which two parts sound **almost the same?**

HAWAIIAN RAINBOWS

Hawaiian Folk Song

Tune up:
```
        5
      3   3
   1        1   1
   G
                5
```

Find the same and different phrases.
How will knowing which phrases are the same or different
help you learn the song?

Ha - wai - ian   rain - bows, — white clouds roll   by, —

You show your   col - ors —— a - gainst the   sky. —

Ha - wai - ian   rain - bows, — it seems to   me, —

Reach from the   moun - tains —— down to the   sea. —

TINGA LAYO

Calypso Song from
the West Indies

Where in each picture do you see things that repeat?

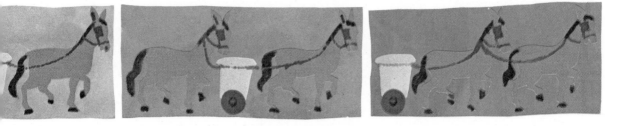

Where in the music do you hear things that repeat?

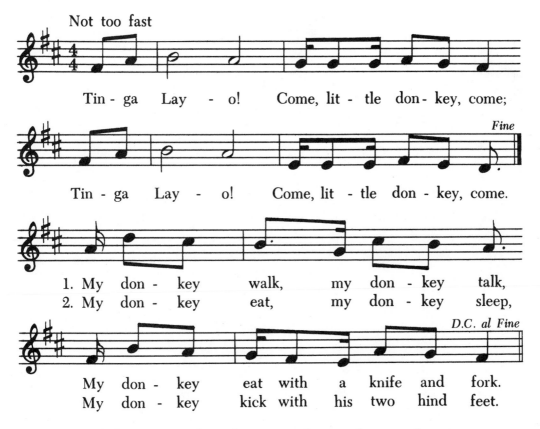

Not too fast

Tin - ga Lay - o! Come, lit - tle don - key, come;

Fine

Tin - ga Lay - o! Come, lit - tle don - key, come.

1. My don - key walk, my don - key talk,
2. My don - key eat, my don - key sleep,

D.C. al Fine

My don - key eat with a knife and fork.
My don - key kick with his two hind feet.

Which of the pictures has the same plan as the song?

BUILDING A CAR

by B. A.

Look at the introduction. Which group chants the shortest sounds?

Which group chants sounds twice as long as the shortest? three times as long?

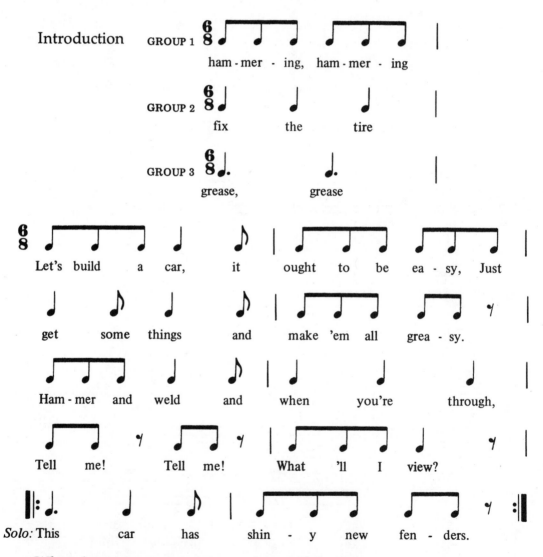

What do you want your car to have? Take turns.
Add your ideas to the chant.

INGONYAMA

Zulu Folk Song

Perform a steady rhythm of short sounds.

Chant the words in relation to these short sounds.

GROUP 1

Like the li - on the li - on the li - on

GROUP 2

The hip - po hip - po hip - po the hip - po

Which animal do you think is the greatest?
Join Group 1 or 2. Sing the song over and over.
Should you sing louder or softer as you repeat the song?
How will you decide?

Some: In - gon - ya - ma, gon - ya - ma, gon - ya - ma!

In - gon - ya - ma, gon - ya - ma, gon - ya - ma!

Others: In - voo - boo, voo - boo, voo - boo, in - voo - boo!

51

WAY DOWN YONDER IN THE BRICKYARD

Written and adapted by
Bessie Jones

Listen to the recording.
When will you move like this?

WILLOWBEE

Traditional Game

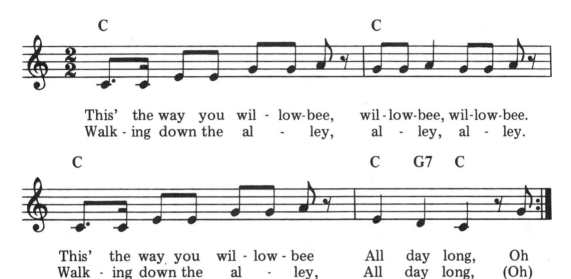

This' the way you wil - low-bee,   wil - low-bee, wil - low-bee.
Walk - ing down the al - ley,   al - ley, al - ley.

This' the way you wil - low - bee   All day long, Oh
Walk - ing down the al - ley,   All day long, (Oh)

This is the way . . .

Walkin' down the alley . . .

SCALES AND ARPEGGIOS

Words and Music by
Richard M. Sherman/Robert B. Sherman

In the first part of this song, C is the tonal center.
Build a major scale starting on C.

When do you sing this scale?

Ev - ery tru - ly cul - tured mu - sic stu - dent knows,

You must learn your scales and your ar - peg - gi - os.

Bring the mu - sic ring - ing from your chest and not your nose,

While you sing your scales and your ar - peg - gi - os.

Do   mi   so   do   do   so   mi   do

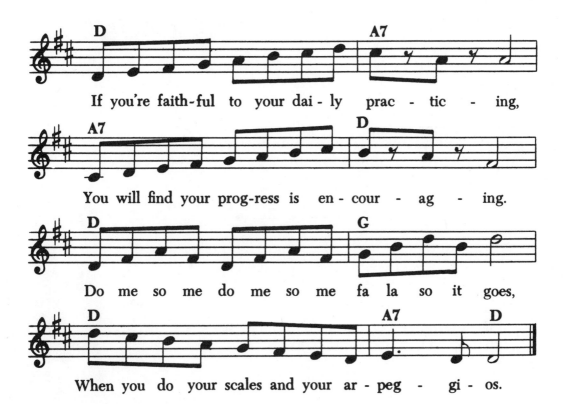

If you're faith-ful to your dai - ly prac - tic - ing,

You will find your prog-ress is en - cour - ag - ing.

Do me so me do me so me fa la so it goes,

When you do your scales and your ar - peg - gi - os.

When did you hear the tonal center change?
Can you build a major scale on the new tonal center?

When do you sing this new scale?

MOTO PERPETUO

from *Matinées Musicales*

by Benjamin Britten

Listen to this music. The orchestra is having fun with scales.
The scale is stated in the introduction. Then various sections
of the orchestra seem to show off as they play scale melodies.

ROW, ROW, ROW YOUR BOAT

Traditional Round

Look at the notes on the staff.
Which note is "1," the tonal center?
Can you find the bell you need to play the sound of "1"?
To do this you need to know the letter names of the notes on
the staff.

C D E F G A B C D E F G

Which is "1"? Play it.
Can you arrange bells to make a major scale?
Start with your tonal center.
Play your scale.
Sing the scale with numbers.
Sing the song with scale numbers.

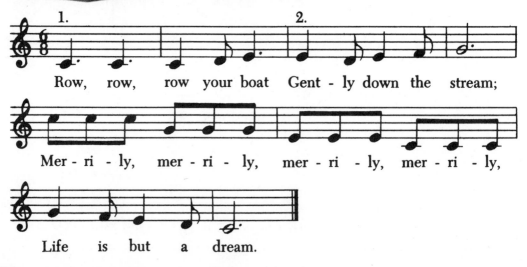

Row, row, row your boat Gent - ly down the stream;

Mer - ri - ly, mer - ri - ly, mer - ri - ly, mer - ri - ly,

Life is but a dream.

THE LITTLE PRINCE

French Folk Song

Tune up:
```
      5
   3     3
1        1
   C
```

Lun- di ma - tin the king, the queen and their prince charm-ing

Came to shake my hand but I was out a farm - ing,

And since I was a - way, the lit - tle prince did say,

"Let's all go home and we'll come back *mar - di.*"

lundi matin—Monday morning	*jeudi*	—Thursday
mardi —Tuesday	*vendredi*—Friday	
mercredi —Wednesday	*samedi* —Saturday	
dimanche—Sunday		

The days of the week are sung in French. Begin and end each
verse using these words.

CHEBOGAH (BEETLE)

Words Adapted

Hungarian Folk Dance

Look at the music. How many phrases do you see?
In some music, phrases are combined to make longer sections.
Listen to the recording and follow the music.
How many sections do you hear?
What helped you know when a new section began?

"Chebogah" is a dance.
The words tell you how to move.
Plan your dance to show the phrases and sections of the music.

In a circle slide to left and don't be slow.
To the right we slide again as back we go.
Forward with a walking step, then back in place.
Skip with elbows joined and then your partner face.
Sideward glide, sideward glide, to the center glide,
Back again, back again, partners side by side.
Faster now, faster now, faster in and out;
Partners swing, partners swing, ending with a shout. Hey!

HUNGARIAN DANCE NO. 1 IN G MINOR

by Johannes Brahms

Follow this chart as you listen to this music.
Can you hear the longer sections of music?

A

1 Theme 1: Rich sound from strings
1 2 3 4 5

2 Repeat

3 Theme 2: Short, fast, whirling sounds

4 Repeat

B

5 Theme 3: Violins slide from low to high to start.

6 Repeat

7 Violins move from high to low to start.

8 Repeat

What happens next in the music?
Can you find it on the chart?

SIM SALA BIM

Danish Folk Song

1. High in a tree a crow - ow - ow,
2. Then came a wick - ed hunt - er a -
3. He shot that poor old crow - ow - ow,

Sim sa - la - bim bam boom, sa - la - doo, sa - la - dim!

High in a tree a crow- ow - ow sat.
Then came a wick- ed hunt - er a - long.
He shot that poor old crow- ow- ow dead.

HOW DO YOU MEASURE UP? (3)

Can you

decide if music is moving in twos or in threes?
find sections in music that are the same? different?
build a major scale?
hear differences between major and minor scales?
perform patterns using short and long sounds?

61

The Fourth Quarter
The Department Store: A Drama

Can you be an actor?
Can you act a believable part?

Scene: A large department store.
Characters: Decide who you will be.

Think about your role.

What do you look like?
How are you dressed?
How do you feel? Shy? Bold? Frightened? Proud?
Why are you in the store?
What will your actions be?

One person should be
the Director.

Action: Begin the drama. Talk with each other. Let others
know who you are and why you are in the store.

Stop action: When the director strikes a finger cymbal. . . . FREEZE. The director signals "continue" to one group. When your group is signaled to continue, go on with your action.

Stop action: An announcement is made over the store intercom: "Ladies and gentlemen. Please proceed calmly to the nearest exit. There is no need for alarm, but we have just discovered that there is a lion loose in the store."

How will you respond to this announcement?

Action:

An Opera

Can you be a singer? Can you act a believable part? Perform "The Department Store" again. This time, sing everything you say. Sing in a way that expresses your ideas and feelings.

HANSEL AND GRETEL

by Engelbert Humperdinck

Do you know the story of Hansel and Gretel? Listen to parts of the story as told in an opera. Tell the other parts in your own words. When you see this sign, ◇ listen. When you see this, ☆ tell the story.

Act 1: Scene 1, in the cottage ◇

Gretel: Su - sy, lit - tle Su - sy, pray what is the news?
Hansel: Su - sy, lit - tle Su - sy, pray what's to be done?

The geese are run - ning bare- foot be - cause they've no shoes.
Who'll give me milk and su - gar, for bread I have none?

The cob - bler has leath - er and plen - ty to spare,
I'll go back to bed and I'll lie there all day,

Why _____ can't he make the poor goose a new pair?
Where there's nought to eat, then there's noth - ing to pay.

☆

64

Gretel: Broth-er come and dance with me, Both my hands I of-fer thee,

Right foot first, Left foot then, Round a-bout and back a-gain.

Act 1: Scene 3, Father returns

Father:

The broom-stick, the broom-stick, why what is it for, why, what is it for?

Act 2: Scene 1, in the forest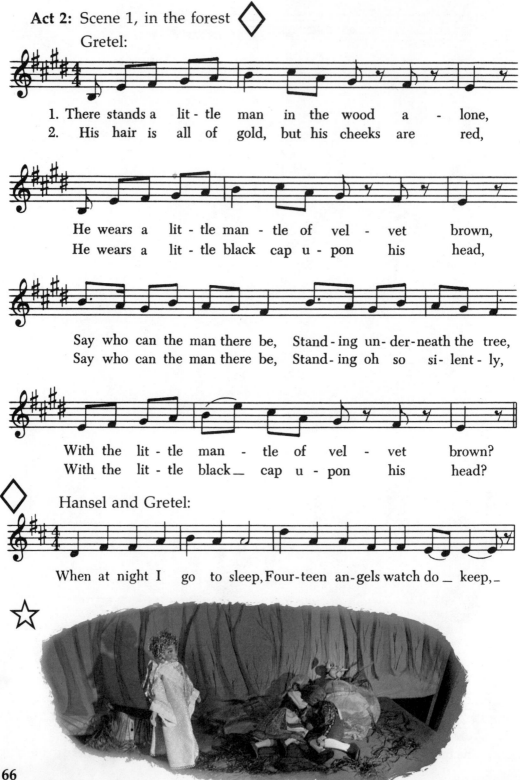

Gretel:

1. There stands a lit - tle man in the wood a - lone,
2. His hair is all of gold, but his cheeks are red,

He wears a lit - tle man - tle of vel - vet brown,
He wears a lit - tle black cap u - pon his head,

Say who can the man there be, Stand - ing un - der-neath the tree,
Say who can the man there be, Stand - ing oh so si - lent - ly,

With the lit - tle man - tle of vel - vet brown?
With the lit - tle black — cap u - pon his head?

Hansel and Gretel:

When at night I go to sleep, Four-teen an - gels watch do — keep, —

66

Act 3: The witch's house

☆

◇ Witch:

So hop, hop, hop, gal-lop, lop, lop! My broom-stick nag, come do not lag!

◇ All:

See, O see the won-der wrought, How the witch her-self was caught,

Now listen to the opera's musical introduction, called the **overture.** The composer introduces you to melodies you hear later in the opera. As you listen, point to the pictures that describe the parts of the opera the composer is using in the overture.

Courtesy, Nicolo Marionettes

WONDERING

Bohemian Folk Song

Each kind of scale has a special sound. Play this scale.

This is a **minor scale.**
Why is a minor scale a good choice for this song?

1. Where are the clouds that were here last night?
2. How far a - way is the dis - tant sky?

Why does the moon give a sil - ver - y light?
How do we know which is you or I?

Who can tell? Who can say?
Who can tell? Who can say?

When will to - mor - row be yes - ter - day?
How man - y miles would be far a - way?

Variations on a Scale
Use Guide Sheets to make up your own variations.

MY OLD HEN

Traditional

My old hen's a good old hen,   She lays eggs for the rail-road men,

Some-times one, some-times two, some-times e-nough for the Pres-i-dent too.

Cluck, old hen, cluck, I   tell you, Cluck, old hen, or I'm gon-na sell you.

Cluck, old hen, cluck, I   say,   Cluck, old hen, or I'll give you a-way.

This melody uses both the **F major** and **F minor** scales.
Play a chord on the first beat of each measure.

When will you play this chord?   C A F   this one?   C A♭ F

69

Explore Harmony on the Autoharp

Choose a tonal center.

E♭   B♭   F   D   G   E   C

Find the major or minor chord on the autoharp that matches the letter name of your tonal center. This is your **I chord**.

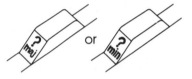

Try these ideas:
- Begin strumming the **I chord.**
- Hold down the chord bar. Gently strike the strings with a mallet.
- Change to another chord, but return often to the **I chord.**

After you have experimented, create a piece for autoharp. Begin and end on the **I chord.**

SKIP TO MY LOU

American Singing Game

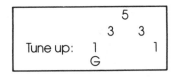

Accompany the song.

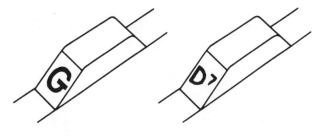

I chord   V chord

Lost my part - ner, what will I do?

Lost my part - ner, what will I do?

Lost my part - ner, what will I do?

Skip to my Lou, my dar - ling.

SUR LE PONT D'AVIGNON

French Folk Song

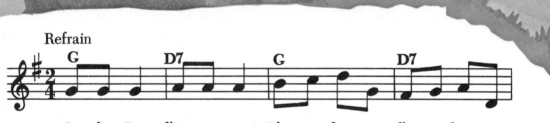

Refrain

Sur le Pont d'A - vi- gnon, L'on y dan - se, l'on y dan - se,

Sur le Pont d'A - vi - gnon, L'on y dan - se tout en rond.

Verse

D.C. al Fine

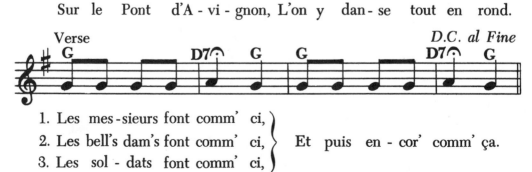

1. Les mes - sieurs font comm' ci,
2. Les bell's dam's font comm' ci, } Et puis en - cor' comm' ça.
3. Les sol - dats font comm' ci,

72

HITORI DE SABISHII
ALONE AND SAD

Japanese Folk Song

Hi - to - ri de sa - bi - shii,
1. By my - self, oh, all a - lone.
2. Let's go to - geth - er, just we two.

Fu - ta - ri de ma - i - ri ma sho.
Sad am I for be - ing all a - lone.
Two can find so man - y things to do.

Add harmony to this song.

Soprano glockenspiel

Alto xylophone

Autoharp: Press two chords down at the same time.

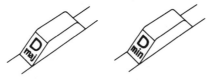

Strum the first beat of each measure.

GET ON BOARD

Spiritual

With strong accent

Get on   board,   lit - tle   chil - dren,   Get on

board,   lit - tle chil - dren, Get on   board,   lit - tle

Fine

chil - dren,   There's room for   man - y   a   more.

The   gos - pel train's a - com - ing, I   hear it   just at

hand; _____   I   hear the car - wheels rum - bling and

D.C. al Fine

roll - ing   through   the   land.   So

Accompany the song.
Use these ideas, or choose others.

clicking wheels: STICKS

engine sounds: SAND BLOCKS

train whistle: BELL

Eb

Play any of these parts on the black keys of the piano.
Experiment by playing on the high keys, then on the
low keys. Which do you like best for this song?

I LOVE THE MOUNTAINS

Traditional

1. F   Dm   Gm   C

I love the moun-tains, I love the roll-ing hills,

2. F   Dm   Gm   C

I love the flow-ers, I love the daf-fo-dils;

3. F   Dm   Gm   C

I love the fire-side when all the lights are low.

F   Dm

Boom - dee - ah - da, Boom - dee - ah - da,

Gm   C

Boom - dee - ah - da, Boom - dee - ah - da.

Explore many ways to play instruments with this song.
Use any of these ideas as you sing the song.

Accompaniments:

Piano or bass xylophone

Piano or alto metallophone

Interlude: Play this after the song is sung. Then sing the song
again.

Use a different sound for the ✗ each time the phrase is repeated.

Follow the instructions on the recording.
Use Guide Sheets.
Use small percussion instruments.
Create music to go with the recorded drum sounds.

WALK TOGETHER CHILDREN

Spiritual

Make up your own harmony part.
Use any of these pitches: A B D E F#
Use this rhythm:

Walk   to - geth - er

Oh,   walk to-geth- er child-ren   don't you get __ wear - y,

Walk   to - geth - er child - ren   don't you get   wear - y.

Oh,   walk to-geth- er child-ren   don't you get __ wear- y.

There's a   great camp meet- ing in the prom-ised land.

THERE'S A LITTLE WHEEL A-TURNIN'

American Folk Song

Group 1: Sing the melody.
Group 2: Add a harmony part.

Wheels   a - turn - in'

1. There's a   lit - tle wheel a - turn - in' in my heart,___
2. There's a   lit - tle song a - sing - in' in my heart,___

There's a   lit - tle wheel a - turn - in' in my heart,
There's a   lit - tle song a - sing - in' in my heart,

In my heart, _____ in my heart, _____
In my heart, _____ in my heart, _____

There's a   lit - tle wheel a - turn - in' in my heart.
There's a   lit - tle song a - sing - in' in my heart.

Making Up a Two-Part Song

THE SNAKE

by Karla Kuskin

Play this part on the bells as the class softly sings. Will you sing staccato or legato sounds? Look at the music. What will help you know?

Si - lent - ly   the   sil - ver   snake goes,

Continue to play the bells and sing softly. Choose someone to make up a song using this poem and these sounds.

A snake slipped through   It moved like a ribbon
the thin green grass   Silent as snow
A silver snake—   I think it smiled
I watched it pass   As it passed my toe.

When the soloist and instruments stop, the class completes the song by singing:

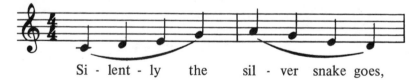

Si - lent - ly   the   sil - ver   snake goes,

In which part of this song were we singing harmony?
Which part had only a melody?

HOW DO YOU MEASURE UP? (4)

Can you
> find same and different sections?
> learn rhythms that use shorter and longer sounds?
> play melodies by following the notes?
> add a harmony part?
> perform a song expressively?

Spring brings the sun where the winter has lain,
Spring brings the comfort of warm gentle rain.
Spring brings song birds from far away.
Winter's gone now, they seem to say.
Springtime has brought us this bright new day.

SOPRANO
GLOCKENSPIEL

BASS
XYLOPHONE

FINGER
CYMBAL

RAINDROPS

Words and Music by Joseph and Nathan Segal

I get to think- ing when it's ___ been rain- ing,

"Why ___ the rain - drops?"

Guess I'm not think- ing like a flow - er's think- ing,

Guess I'm not feel- ing what a tree is feel - ing

In the rain - drops.

Play an **introduction,** an **accompaniment,** and a **coda.**
Begin with the sound of rain.

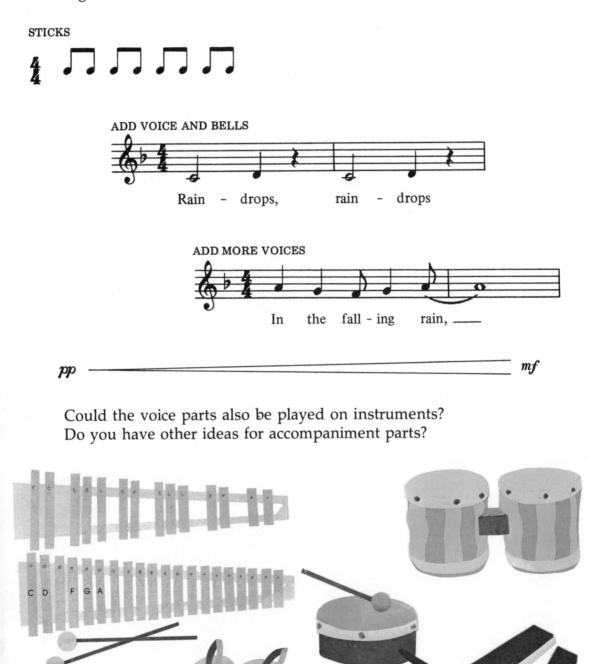

STICKS

ADD VOICE AND BELLS

Rain - drops,　　rain - drops

ADD MORE VOICES

In　the　fall - ing　rain, ___

pp ———————————————————————————— *mf*

Could the voice parts also be played on instruments?
Do you have other ideas for accompaniment parts?

C D F G A

MORE MUSIC TO EXPLORE

Perform by Singing and Playing

TO THE KORNER KRINKLESTEIN

by B. A.

Use your voice in special ways. Follow the leader.

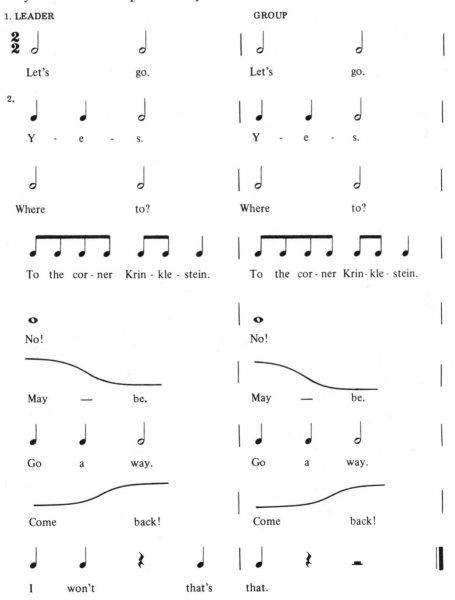

Learn to Sing Special Parts
TONGO

Polynesian Folk Song

This song is sung in two parts: a leader and an echo group.
How can you tell if the two parts are sung in harmony?

Leader: Ton - go __ Group: Ton - go __ Leader: Jim-nee bye __ bye __ oh

Group: Jim - nee bye __ bye __ oh Leader: Ton - go __ Group: Ton - go __

Leader: Oom ba de kim bye oh Group: Oom ba de kim bye oh

Leader: Ooh - a - lay, Group: Ooh - a - lay,

Leader: Mah - le - ka - ah lo way.

Group: Mah - le - ka - ah lo way.

86

THE GOAT

Traditional Folk Song

This song is performed in two parts.
Group 1 sings the first melody pattern.
Group 2 echoes the pattern while Group 1 holds the last tone.
How can you tell if these two parts are sung in harmony?

1. One day a goat _____ was feel - ing fine, _____
2. Sing a - di - os _____ but not good - bye, _____

Ate three red shirts _____ right off the line. _____
That goat was down _____ but not to die. _____

Jack took a stick, _____ gave him a whack, _____
He gave one yell _____ as though in pain, _____

And laid him on _____ the rail - road track. _____
Coughed up those shirts _____ and flagged the train. _____

TRAIL TO MEXICO

American Folk Song

Look at the music. Listen to the recording.
Can you follow part 1 and part 2 on your page of music?

Now can you sing part 1 and part 2?

Part 1

I made up my — mind ——————

Part 2

I made up my mind —

in the ear - ly day, ——————

— in the ear - ly day, —

To leave my home ——————

— To leave my home —

and __ change my way, _____

— and change my way, __

To leave my na - - - -

— To leave my land __

tive land for a - while, _____

— for just a - while, __

89

To trav - el west _____

To trav - el west_

for ___ man - y a mile. _____

for man- y a mile.

AH, POOR BIRD

Words Adapted

Old English Melody

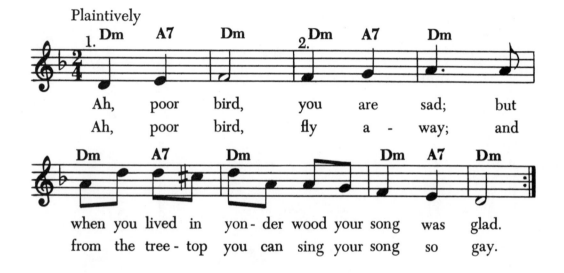

Plaintively

Dm A7 Dm Dm A7 Dm

Ah, poor bird, you are sad; but
Ah, poor bird, fly a - way; and

Dm A7 Dm Dm A7 Dm

when you lived in yon - der wood your song was glad.
from the tree - top you can sing your song so gay.

Here is another way to sing in harmony.

Group 1 sings the melody.

Group 2 repeats the first two measures all through the song.

Ah, poor bird.

Sing again. This time, Group 2 uses "loo" instead of words.
Which do you think sounds better with the melody—the repeated
words or "loo"?

91

Peter Piper

Traditional

Can you clap the rhythm pattern of the words?
Follow the signs that show

the shortest sound.

sounds that move with the beat.

a silence that lasts for a beat.

Pe - ter Pi – per   picked a peck of   pick - led   pep-pers!

Eh?   Eh?   What's that ya'   say?

Now perform the chant.

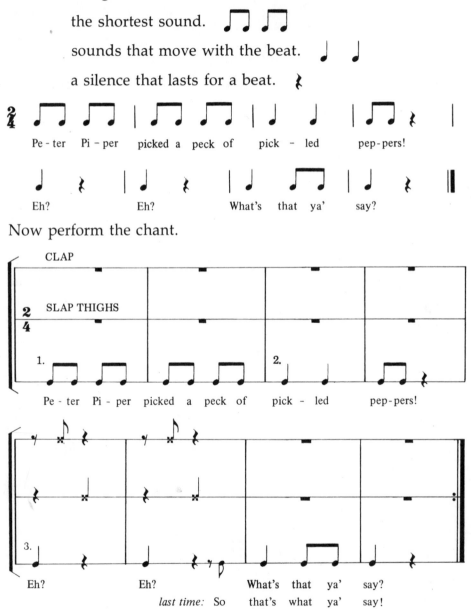

Perform the chant three times. Each time, get louder.
Then perform the chant as a canon.

Canoe Song

American Indian

My pad - dle's keen and bright, Flash - ing with sil - ver.

Fol - low the wild goose flight, Dip, dip, and swing.

Create harmony using just one melody.

How can the same melody sung by two people create harmony?

MICHAEL, ROW THE BOAT ASHORE

Spiritual

With feeling

LEAD SINGER

1. Mi - chael, row   the boat a - shore,
2. Mi - chael's boat's   a mu - sic   boat,

BACKUP GROUP

Hal - le - lu - jah!
Hal - le - lu - jah!

LEAD SINGER

Mi - chael, row   the boat a - shore,
Mi - chael's boat's   a mu - sic   boat,

BACKUP GROUP

Hal - le - lu - jah!
Hal - le - lu - jah!

3. Michael, row the boat ashore, Hallelujah! *(2 times)*
4. Sister, help to trim the sail, Hallelujah! *(2 times)*
5. Michael, row the boat ashore, Hallelujah! *(2 times)*

94

Form a Special Performing Group

One person is the lead singer.   Others are the back-up group.

Sing "Michael, Row the Boat Ashore."

Some members of the back-up group may add a harmony part while others continue to sing the melody.

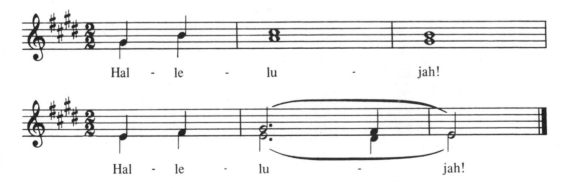

When is the harmony part the same as the melody?
When is it different?

AT THE GATE OF HEAVEN

Words Adapted   Spanish-American Folk Song

Part 1

1. At the gate of Heav'n   ti - ny shoes they are giv - ing

Part 2

1. At the gate of Heav'n ti - ny shoes they are

To the lit - tle bare - foot-ed an - gels there liv - ing.

giv - ing   To the lit - tle bare - foot-ed an - gels there

Refrain

Slum - ber, my lit - tle one,

liv - ing.   Slum - ber, my lit - tle one,

Slum - ber, my ni - ño, a - rru, a - rru.

Slum - ber my ni - ño, a - rru, a - rru.

CHILDSONG

Words and Music
by Neil Diamond

A good singing group sings with
- correct rhythm
- correct melody
- expression.

1. Perform this song with the correct rhythm.
    Tap the short sounds shown below and chant
    the words. Listen to the recording to
    check your performance.

Weep - ing sky, we bring the sun to make you

glad and fill you with the day.

2. Perform the melody with the correct pitches.
    Most of the song uses only these five pitches.

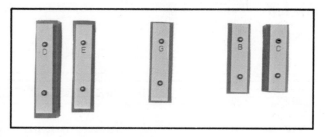

Can you sing the first phrase?
Listen to the recording to check your performance.

3. Perform with expression.
    At what tempo will you sing? fast? slow? medium?

    Will you sing *legato*?   or *staccato*?

    Will you sing loudly or softly?
    Will you change from loud to soft or soft to loud?

Weep - ing sky, we bring the sun

To make you glad and fill you with the day. ___

Qui - et tree, we have the wind

To make you dance and fill you with our play. ___

And you shall be glad ___ and you shall dance. __

And you shall come to hear our song

And learn its tune be - fore it fades a - way. ___

GILLY'S BAND

Bring instruments from home. Play in this special band.

Who will play the shortest sounds? sounds twice as long as the shortest sound? four times as long? eight times?

AT A GEORGIA CAMP MEETING

Words and Music by Kerry Mills

Play the rhythm parts for "Gilly's Band" with this song.

When those hot mu - si-cians be-gan to play____ ____ Mu-sic hap-py and gay, _____ They were danc-ing a-way. _____ Yes, in - deed, the rhy-thm was sure. O. K. Soon your wor - ry left in a hur - ry Down at the Geor-gia Camp Meet-ing ho - li - day.

AL HASELA

Biblical Text   Hasidic Tune

Joyously

Al ha - se - la haḥ, haḥ, al ha - se - la

haḥ, haḥ, haḥ, Al ha - se - la haḥ, haḥ, v'

1.   2.

yë - tsu ma - yim ḥa - yim, ḥa - yim. ___

La la la la la la la la

la La la la la la haḥ, haḥ, haḥ,

la la la la la hah, hah, hah, La la

la la la la la la la la la la la.

Accompany the song by clapping the short sounds.

Tap your knee with your right hand,
then tap the bottom of your left hand.

Now move your hands away from your knee.
Beat the air instead of your knee.

Play this pattern.

Play the same pattern by gently tapping on a cymbal.

Add another instrumental part.

Perform the song using both instruments.

TURN THE GLASSES OVER

American Singing Game

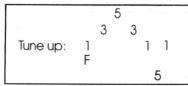

Learn accompaniment parts for this song.

Strum autoharp:

Play this on bells or piano:

Heartily

I've been to Haar - lem, I've been to Do - ver,

I've trav - eled this wide world all o - ver,

O - ver, o - ver, three times o - ver,

Drink what you have to drink and turn the glas- ses o - ver.

Sail - ing east, sail - ing west,

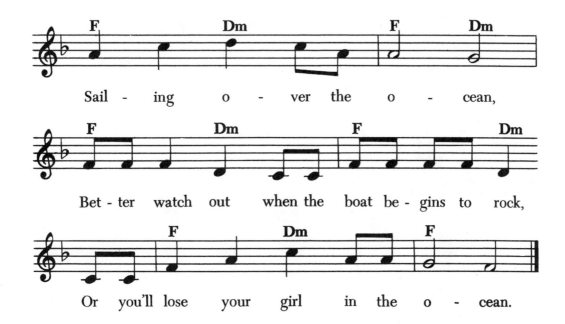

Sail - ing   o - ver   the   o - cean,

Bet - ter   watch   out   when the   boat be - gins   to   rock,

Or   you'll   lose   your   girl   in   the   o - cean.

You the Accompanist

Follow the instructions on the recording.
Use Guide Sheets.
Make up and play accompaniments to songs.
How can your accompaniment help express the ideas in a:

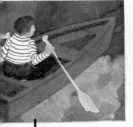
boat song?

spring song?

game song?

train song?

Plan to create only one or two accompaniments at one time.
Then use the recording again to create other accompaniments.

CHERRY BLOOM

Japanese Folk Song

Gently

Cher - ry   bloom,   cher - ry   bloom,
Sa - ku - ra   Sa - ku - ra

Gent - ly sway - ing   in the ___ air,
Ya - yo - i   no   so - ra ___ wa

Sweet the   fra - grance ev - ery - where,
Mi - wa - ta - su   ka - gi - ri

Pet - als   soft   and   col - ors ___ bright,
Ka - su - mi   ka   ku - mo ___ ka

Float - ing   clouds   that   seem   to ___ say:
Ni - o - i   zo   i - zu - ru

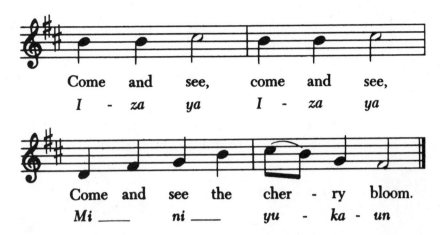

Come and see, come and see,
I - za ya I - za ya

Come and see the cher - ry bloom.
Mi ____ ni ____ yu - ka - un

Notice the sounds of the **koto** as you listen to the recording.
Japanese folk songs are often accompanied by this ancient
string instrument.
You can suggest the sound of the koto on the autoharp or violin.
Pluck the F# and G strings in this rhythm.

F#   G   F#   G

My Nature Song

"Cherry Bloom" uses only five different tones. Many songs from
Japan use only five tones. Make up your own five-tone song
about nature. You may write your own poem or use one of these.

Cherry blossoms, yes
    They're beautiful . . .
    But tonight
Don't miss the moon!

       So-in

Little Bird flitting
    twittering, trying
    to fly . . .
My, aren't you busy!

      Basho

RAIN CHANT

Translated by Natalie Curtis Burlin

Use the sounds of rattles to accompany this chant.
Play the rattles different ways to make different sounds.

slowly turning   rapid shaking   bumping on opposite hand

SOLO   Far as man can see,
GROUP   Comes the rain,
        Comes the rain with me.
SOLO   From the rain mount,
        Rain mount far away,
GROUP   Comes the rain,
        Comes the rain with me.
SOLO   O'er the corn,
        O'er the tall corn.
GROUP   Comes the rain
        Comes the rain with me.
SOLO   Mid the lightning's,
        Mid the lightning's zigzag
        Mid the lightning's flashing.
GROUP   Comes the rain,
        Comes the rain with me.
SOLO   Mid the swallows,
        Mid the swallows blue
        Chirping glad together.
GROUP   Comes the rain,
        Comes the rain with me.

How can you use changes in loudness
and softness to express the ideas
of this chant?

LAND OF THE SILVER BIRCH

Canadian Folk Song

1. Land of the sil - ver birch, home of the bea - ver,
2. Down in the for - est, deep in the low - lands,
3. High on a rock - y ledge, I'll build a wig - wam,

Where still the might - y moose wan - ders at will,
My heart cries out for thee, hills of the north.
Close by the wa - ter's edge, si - lent and still.

Refrain

Blue lake and rock - y shore, I will re - turn once more.

Boom de de boom boom, Boom de de boom boom,

Boom de de boom boom, Boom ___ boom boom. ___

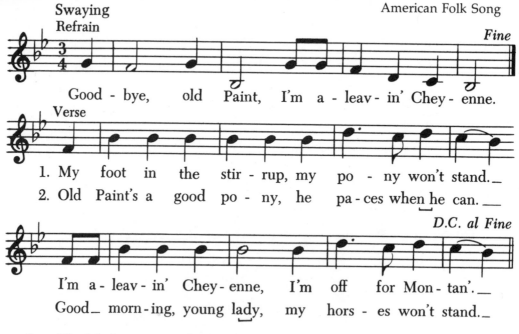

GOODBYE, OLD PAINT

American Folk Song

Swaying
Refrain

Fine

Good - bye, old Paint, I'm a - leav - in' Chey - enne.

Verse

1. My foot in the stir - rup, my po - ny won't stand. __
2. Old Paint's a good po - ny, he pa - ces when he can. __

D.C. al Fine

I'm a - leav - in' Chey - enne, I'm off for Mon - tan'. __
Good __ morn - ing, young lady, my hors - es won't stand. __

3. Oh, hitch up your hosses and feed 'em some hay,
   And seat yourself by me, as long as you stay.

4. I am a-riding old Paint, I am a-leading old Dan,
   I'm goin' to Montan' for to throw the hoolihan.

Collected, adapted and arranged by John A. Lomax and Alan Lomax.
TRO-Copyright 1934, renewed © 1962 Ludlow Music, Inc. Used by permission.

Repeat these parts many times as you sing the song.

Part 1 - TONE BLOCKS

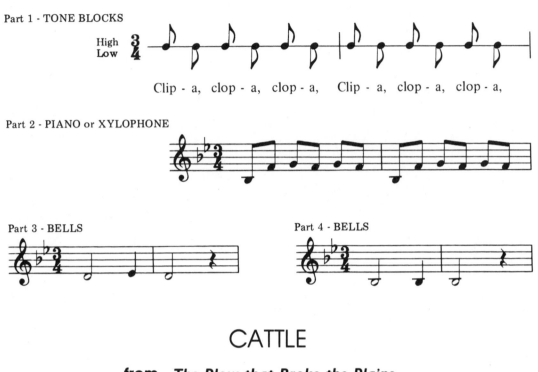

Clip - a, clop - a, clop - a, Clip - a, clop - a, clop - a,

Part 2 - PIANO or XYLOPHONE

Part 3 - BELLS

Part 4 - BELLS

CATTLE

from *The Plow that Broke the Plains*

by Virgil Thomson

Cowboys often spend many lonely hours herding cattle. To pass the time, they sing songs about their horses, homes, and the cattle trail.

Can you hear three different cowboy melodies in this music? Different instruments take turns playing the three melodies.

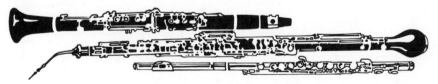

Other instruments play an accompaniment to add harmony. Sometimes the strings pluck an "um pah pah" pattern. Sometimes they play in arpeggios.

When the strings play the melodies, the full orchestra is the accompaniment.

Describe Music

HILL AND GULLY RIDER

American Folk Song

```
                    5
              3   3
Tune up:  1           1   1
                          5
```

Can you find the tonal center by looking at the music?
When you tune up, which pitch will be 1?

Play the tonal center each time you sing the words
"hill and gully."

Hill and gul - ly rid - er,   hill and   gul - ly,

Hill and gul - ly rid - er,   hill and gul - ly,   When you're

feel - in' low down, Hill and gul - ley, Nev - er
let it keep you down, Hill and gul - ly. As you
go a - long you sing a song, Hill and gul - ley, As you
go a - long you sing a song, Hill and gul - ley.

(Interlude)

LET'S GO FLY A KITE

Music by Richard M. Sherman
Words by Robert B. Sherman

Listen to the recording.

One person chooses to move with:
  the heavy and light beats,
              or
  the melody,
              or
  the sounds of voices or instruments.

Others watch, and guess what the dancer
was describing.

Let's   go   fly   a   kite

Up   to   the   high - est   height!

Let's   go   fly   a   kite

And   send   it   soar - ing

Up through the at - mos - phere,

Up where the air is clear.

Oh, let's go _____ fly a

kite! _____

Describe Music Through Movement - Dance a Waltz

EVOLUTIONS

by Henrik Badings

Is this a waltz?
Does it remind you of the
"Music Box Waltz" in any way?

Who might dance this music?
How would they move?

MUSIC BOX WALTZ

by Dimitri Shostakovitch

How does a waltz move?

━━ ── ━━ ──

or

━━ ── ── ━━ ── ──

or

━━ ── ── ──

Make up a waltz step.
Take big steps on the accents.
Take short steps on the other beats.

THREE TO GET READY

by Dave Brubeck

One for the money,
Two for the show

Three to get ready
And four to go!

Did the composer choose a good
title for his music? Why?

Tap the rhythm as you listen.

116

The Circus
Georges Seurat
Jeu de Paume, Paris
SCALA, New York/Florence

DANCE OF THE COMEDIANS

from *The Bartered Bride*

by Bedrich Smetana

Listen to the "Dance of the Comedians."
Close your eyes as you listen.
What kinds of dances do you imagine?

Do you hear different sections in the music?
Do the different sections make you think of
different kinds of dances?

Are any sections repeated?
Do your imaginary dancers
repeat their dance steps?

Try dancing your own dance.
Your dance may follow the rhythm
or the melody of the music.

Divide into four groups; each group
may plan a different section.

Plan a grand finale for your dance.
Repeat your dances together for an exciting
ending to the music.

DREAM DUST

Words by Langston Hughes

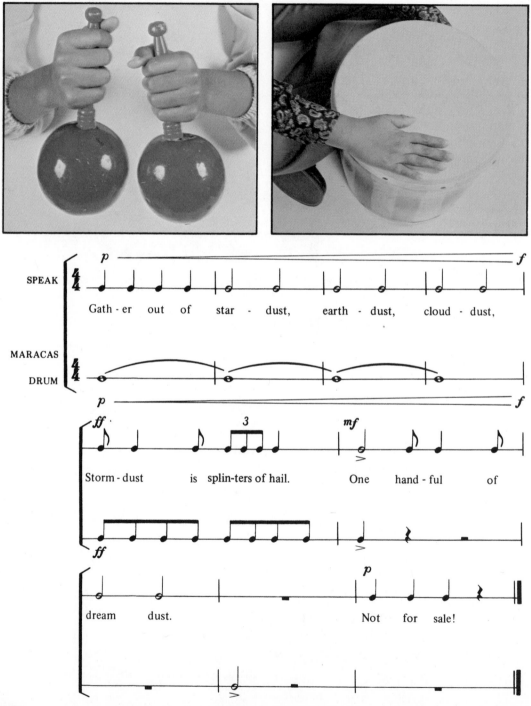

Perform this poem.

Use   speech   sounds   movement

Work in three groups.
Select three "Music Readers." They are responsible for telling
others how to perform this work.

Music Reader 1 teaches how to speak the poem.

Music Reader 2 teaches the accompaniment to the players.

Music Reader 3 teaches the movements.

Did Music Readers 1 and 2 understand the score?
Did they read it correctly?

Movement Directions

Gather out of star-dust,   reach high and gather stars

_____

earth-dust,   reach low and gather dust

_____

cloud-dust,   reach high and make large
                   gathering motion

_____

storm-dust and splinters   spin around, then sit on floor
of hail,

_____

One handful of dream dust   raise hand to sky

_____

Not for sale   clench fist and draw back to
                    chest.

119

IT'S A SMALL WORLD

Words and Music by
Richard M. Sherman
and Robert B. Sherman

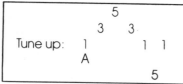

March tempo

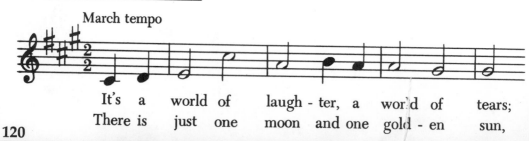

It's a world of laugh-ter, a world of tears;
There is just one moon and one gold-en sun,

It's a world of hopes and a world of fears.
And a smile means friend-ship to ev - ery one.

There's so much that we share, and it's time we're a - ware,
Though the moun-tains di - vide and the o - ceans are wide,

Fine

It's a small world af - ter all. _____
It's a small world af - ter all. _____

It's a small world af - ter all,

It's a small world af - ter all,

It's a small world af - ter all,

D.C. al Fine

It's a small, small world. _____

PUMPKINEATER'S LITTLE FUGUE

Robert McBride

Peter, Peter, Pumpkineater
Had a wife and couldn't keep her.
Put her in a pumpkin shell
And there he kept her very well.

Learn to play this song on the black keys of the piano.
Follow this "backwards" score.

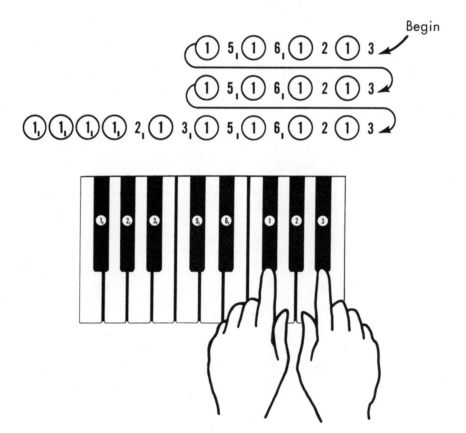

The left index finger always plays 1.
The right index finger must follow the other numbers.

Listen to a composition that uses this melody.
What kind of instruments are playing? Brass? String? Percussion?

Explore the Instruments of the String Family

Many people begin learning to play the violin in school.
Ask a violin student to show your class a violin.
Ask questions about the . . .

tuning pegs
four strings
fingerboard
bridge
chin rest
hand and finger positions
bow—frog, tip

Ask the student to play this violin part while your class sings
"Come Boating with Me."

AIR

from *Suite No. 3 in D Major*

by J. S. Bach

Listen to a composition for string instruments.

Create Music
Search for Sounds

Listen in special ways.
You might hear these sounds . . .

- in your home
- on city streets
- in the country
- in your classroom

Say hello to four friends. Decide whether they answer with **high** or **low** sounds.

Slide on something. What kind of a sound did you make?

Listen to feet moving **evenly, unevenly.**

Think about a sound that is farther away than all others.

Place your ear close to something as it makes a sound.

Think about a sound that is coming toward you. What did you hear as it came close and passed by?

Make an echo.

Climb to a high place and describe a sound below. Sit under something and describe a sound above.

Can you use instruments to suggest some of the special sounds you heard? Share your ideas with the class.

124

THE JUNGLE

by B. A.

_f_ The cat,———— the cat, ————

He crouches, a tiger, so flat ————

He ～SLIDES～ ～SLIDES～

and slinks ∿∿∿

In the jungle by the kitchen sink!

_p_ The mouse,————the mouse, ————

Skiddles to a hole in the house. ∿∿∿

He fearfully blinks,——————

But is safe he thinks ——————

In the jungle by the kitchen sink!

Everyone could speak the poem together.

Someone might play this accompaniment on piano or bells:

Here is a part for a solo performer. Each time you see _____
make up a tune in rhythm with the poem. Use these sounds.

C   D   E   F♯   G♯   A♯   C

The Artist

Seascape, 1947 Alexander Calder
Collection of the Whitney Museum of
American Art. Gift of the Howard and
Jean Lipman Foundation, Inc.
(photo by Geoffrey Clements)

Boxing, 1914 Alexander Archipenko
Collection, The Museum of Modern Art,
New York.

Here are two examples of sculpture.
How does each express movement?
Create a "living sculpture."
Work in pairs. One person is the artist, the other the clay.
The artist shapes the clay by moving arms, legs, head, and body
into position.
The sculpture is "frozen" in place.
The sculpture then becomes a moving sculpture.

Musicians accompany the movements. Choose from sounds of:
drum
tambourine
finger cymbals
large cymbals
wood block
maracas

VARIATION ON A KOREAN FOLK SONG

by John Barnes Chance

Listen to a band playing this music.

Theme: The melody begins with a clarinet playing low sounds. Other instruments join in playing a drone.

Variation: This time, one group of instruments begins the melody. Another follows close behind.

What other differences between the theme and variation can you hear?

Play a piece using only wooden instruments.

Some people should hold the instruments while another person plays the piece.

Play this rhythm pattern. Use each instrument sound at least one time.

How could you vary your piece?

A Composition for the Autoharp

Cut a sheet of paper to fit
under the strings of an autoharp.

Draw along each string with a pencil
to make a score sheet.

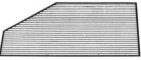

Use a colored pen to draw your ideas
on the score. You might use:

short plucking sounds

the specific pitch of a plucked string

strums going down and up

What other sounds might you show?

Place the score under the autoharp strings again.
Perform your piece by following your score.

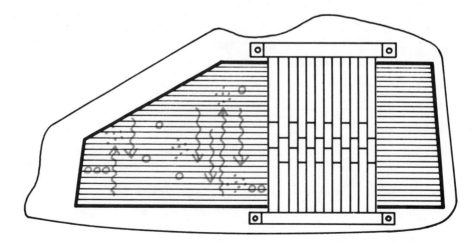

A Melody for the Autoharp

You can play melodies on the autoharp as well as chords.
Prepare a sheet of paper as you did on page 128.
Find these three strings near the middle of the autoharp:

G   A   B

Draw a line along these three strings to make your score.
Copy those dots on your score sheet.

Who's That Yonder?
autoharp score

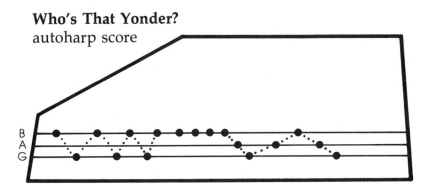

Pluck each dot to play the melody.
You will need to remember the rhythm of the melody
and make each sound longer and shorter as needed.

FOR HEALTH AND STRENGTH

Traditional Round

Play a score for this song.

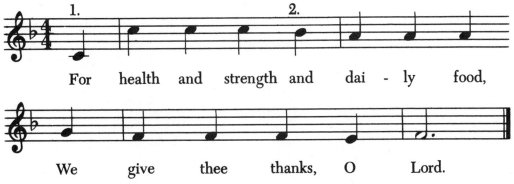

For   health   and   strength and   dai - ly   food,

We   give   thee   thanks,   O   Lord.

NIGHT HERDING SONG

Cowboy Song

Easily

1. Go slow, lit - tle do - gies, stop mill - in' a - round;
2. Lay down, lit - tle do - gies, and when you've laid down

I'm tired of your rov - in' all o - ver the ground.
Just stretch your-selves out for there's plen - ty of ground.

There's grass where you're stand - in', so feed kind of slow;
Stay put, lit - tle do - gies, for I'm aw - ful tired;

You don't have for - ev - er to be on the go.
If you get a - way I am sure to be fired.

Move slow, lit - tle do - gies, move slow, _____
Lay down, lit - tle do - gies, lay down, _____

Hi - o, hi - o, _____ hi - o. _____

Create instrumental parts for this cowboy song.
Use any of these pitches:

F   G   A   C   D

Each part must be only one measure long.

Plan a rhythm for your part that uses

the shortest sounds

or long sounds

or both long and short sounds
in an **uneven** pattern.

Play the parts at the same time as an accompaniment for the song.
Repeat each part over and over throughout the song.

131

A Theater Production:
THE UGLY DUCKLING

Words and Music
by Frank Loesser

Sing . . . act . . . dance . . . play instruments.
Perform your production for others.
First, create an overture and finale for "The Ugly Duckling."

Use a guiro for duck sounds.
What other percussion sounds
might you add?
Arrange all your ideas to create an overture and a finale.
Now look over the music. Decide who will perform each
part.

SINGER: There once was an ugly duckling
With feathers all stubby and brown
And the other birds in so many words
Said "Get out of town.
Get out! Get out! Get out of town."

CHORUS

And he went with a quack and a wad-dle and a

quack in a flur-ry of ei-der-down.

BELL INTERLUDE

SINGER: **The poor little ugly duckling**
Went wandering far and near
But at every place they said to his face
"Now, get out of here!
Get out! Get out! Get out of here!"

And he went with a quack and a wad-dle and a

quack and a ve-ry un-hap-py tear.

BELL INTERLUDE

PART 1

All thru the win-ter time he hid him-self a-way. A-

PART 2

All thru the win-ter time he hid him-self a-way. A-

shamed to show his face, A-fraid of what oth-ers might say.

shamed to show his face, A-fraid of what oth-ers might say.

All thru the win-ter in his lone-ly clump of weed. 'Til a

All thru the win-ter in his lone-ly clump of weed. 'Til a

PARTS 1 AND 2

flock of swans spied him there and ver-y soon a-gree, "You're a

ver-y fine swan in-deed!"

UGLY DUCKLING: Swan? Me a swan? Aw . . . go on!
CHORUS *(speak)*: You're a swan! Take a look at yourself in the lake and you'll see!
ONE SPEAKER: And he looked and he saw, and he said:
UGLY DUCKLING: Why, it's ME! I am a swan! Whee!
UGLY DUCKLING: I'm not such an ugly duckling
No feathers all stubby and brown.
For in fact these birds
In so many words said
Tsk! The best in town,
Tsk! The best, tsk, tsk, the best,
Tsk! Tsk! the best in town.

CHORUS

Not a quack, not a quack, not a wad-dle or a quack, But a

glide and a whis-tle and a snow-y white back and a

head so no-ble and high! Say who's an ug-ly

duck-ling? Not I!

Special Times
BETWEEN BIRTHDAYS
by Ogden Nash

My birthdays take so long to start
They come along a year apart.
It's worse than waiting for a bus
I fear I used to fret and fuss
But now, when by impatience vexed
Between one birthday and the next
I think of all that I have seen
That keeps on happening in between,
The songs I've heard, the things I've done,
Make my "unbirthdays" not so "un"!

THE UNBIRTHDAY SONG

Words and Music by Mack David,
Al Hoffman, and Jerry Livingston

1. A ver-ry mer-ry un-birth-day to you, to you,
2. A ver-ry mer-ry un-birth-day to us, to us,

A ver-ry mer-ry un-birth-day to you, to you,
A ver-ry mer-ry un-birth-day to us, to us,

It's great to drink to some-one and I guess that you will do,
If there are no ob-jec-tions let it be u-nan-i-mous,

A ver-y mer-ry un-birth-day to you. _____
A ver-y mer-ry un-birth-day to us. _____

HALLOWE'EN

Words by Harry Behn

Music by John Wood

Mysteriously

1. To - night is the night when dead leaves fly
2. To - night is the night when leaves do sound
3. To - night is the night when pump - kins stare

Like witch - es on switch - es a - cross the sky,
Like gnomes in their homes far be - neath the ground,
Through brown sheaves and leaves al - most ev - ery - where,

When elf and sprite flit through the night,
When spooks and trolls creep out of holes
When ghoul and ghost and gob - lin host

On a moon - y sheen, on a moon - y sheen.
Dark and moss - y green, dark and moss - y green.
Dance a - round their queen, for it's Hal - low - e'en!

THE BANSHEE!

by B. A.

A banshee is a ghost,
She howls and wallows
As she mysteriously moves
Through the old dark hollow!

She comes in the night
And peers from room to room
Then returns at dawn
To the dark side of the moon.

Make up music to suggest the sounds of the banshee. Use an autoharp, a guitar, or the strings of the piano. Discover unusual sounds on your instrument by playing it in new ways. Use a plastic pick or a metal key and make scraping sounds. Tap the strings with a mallet. What other ways can you find?

When you have found interesting sounds, put them together as an accompaniment for the poem. Play your music as the class speaks the poem, or play it as a solo.

BANSHEE

by Henry Cowell

Henry Cowell was an American composer who explored new ways of making music. Listen to his music called "Banshee."

Can you decide what instrument he used? How do you think the performer makes the unusual sounds you hear?

Why do you think the composer's new sounds on a familiar instrument are good ways to express the banshee?

HARVEST SONG

Traditional Words

Danish Song

1. Out in the mead - ows the grain has been cra - dled,
2. Soon we shall har - vest the corn which is ri - pened;

Rye and wheat are stacked and soon the hay is in the barn.
Let us count our bless - ings as the grain is gath - ered in.

Trees have been shak - en and fruit has been gath - ered,
So in the full - ness of boun - ti - ful har - vest,

Home-ward now we wend our way up - on the fi - nal load.
Let us keep an o - pen heart for those who are in need.

Refrain

Glad - ness on ev - ery hand, Games and dance through-out the land;

Sing - ing mer - ri - ly we bind the hap - py har - vest wreath.

THERE ARE MANY FLAGS IN MANY LANDS

Words by M. H. Howliston

Composer Unknown

In march time

There are man - y flags in man - y lands,

There are flags of ev - ery hue;

But there is no flag, how - ev - er grand,

Like our own Red, White, — and — Blue.

Then hur - rah for the flag, our coun - try's flag,

Its stripes and white stars, too;

For there is no flag in an-y land

Like our own Red, White,— and — Blue.

HANUKAH

Words Adapted

Jewish Folk Song

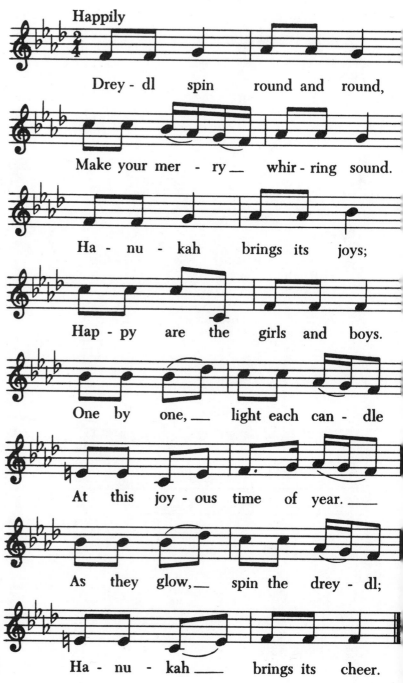

Happily

Drey - dl spin round and round,

Make your mer - ry — whir - ring sound.

Ha - nu - kah brings its joys;

Hap - py are the girls and boys.

One by one, — light each can - dle

At this joy - ous time of year. —

As they glow, — spin the drey - dl;

Ha - nu - kah — brings its cheer.

AFRICAN NOEL

Liberian Folk Song

Play this part as you sing the first two staffs of the music.

When does it become a harmony part? When is it a melody part? Where could we use this part again in the song?

Sing No - el, sing No - el, No - el No - el. ____

Sing No - el, sing No - el, No - el No - el. ____

Sing we all No - el, sing we all No - el,

Sing we all No - el, sing we all No - el.

Sing No - el, sing No - el, No - el No - el. ____

Sing No - el, sing No - el, No - el No - el. ____

DECK THE HALLS

Old Welsh Air
Traditional Words

In what ways do you and your family celebrate special holidays? This carol tells about ways people celebrated Christmas long ago. Yuletide is another word for Christmas. The Yule log was a huge log that was placed in the fireplace on Christmas Eve. It burned all through the twelve days of the holiday season.

Gaily

1. Deck the halls with boughs of hol - ly,
2. See the blaz - ing Yule be - fore us,
3. Fast a - way the old year pass - es,

Fa la la la la la la la la.

'Tis the sea - son to be jol - ly,
Strike the harp and join the cho - rus,
Hail the new, ye lads and lass - es,

Fa la la la la la la la la.

Don we now our gay ap - par - el,
Fol - low me in mer - ry mea - sure,
Sing we joy - ous all to - geth - er,

Fa la la la la la la la la.

Troll the an - cient Yule - tide car - ol,
While I tell of Yule - tide trea - sure,
Heed - less of the wind and weath - er,

Fa la la la la la la la la.

'TWAS IN THE MOON OF WINTERTIME

Words by J. E. Middleton

Huron Indian Carol

Use this soft drum accompaniment as you sing:

1. 'Twas in the moon of win - ter - time
2. With - in a lodge of bro - ken bark
3. Ye chil - dren of the for - est free,

when all the birds had fled,
the ten - der Babe was found.
ye sons of Man - i - tou,

That might - y Git - chi Man - i - tou
A rag - ged robe of rab - bit skin
The Ho - ly Child of earth and heav'n

sent an - gel choirs in - stead.
en - wrapped His beau - ty round.
is born to - day for you.

Be - fore their light the stars grew dim,
And as the hunt - er braves drew nigh,
Come kneel be - fore the ra - diant Boy

and won - d'ring hunt - ers heard the hymn: ___
the an - gel song rang loud and high: ___
who brings you beau - ty, peace, and joy; ___

Refrain

Je - sus, your King, is born; Je - sus is

born! *In ex - cel - sis glo - ri - a!*

Play a solo drum part before you sing each new verse. Continue playing the beat, but slowly change the loudness and softness of your playing. *p* ——————— *ff* ———————— *p*

THE LITTLE DRUMMER BOY

Words and Music by Katherine Davis,
Henry Onorati, and Harry Simeone

Moderately

1. Come they told me pa-rum pum pum pum, ___
2. Lit - tle Ba - by pa-rum pum pum pum, ___
3. Mar - y nod - ded pa-rum pum pum pum, ___

A new born King to see, pa-rum pum pum pum, ___
I am a poor boy too, pa-rum pum pum pum, ___
The Ox and Lamb kept time, pa-rum pum pum pum, ___

Our fin - est gifts we bring pa-rum pum pum pum, ___
I have no gift to bring pa-rum pum pum pum, ___
I played my drum for him pa-rum pum pum pum, ___

To lay be - fore the King pa-rum pum pum pum,
That's fit to give our King pa-rum pum pum pum,
I played my best for him pa-rum pum pum pum,

148

rum pum pum pum, rum pum pum pum. _____
rum pum pum pum, rum pum pum pum. _____
rum pum pum pum, rum pum pum pum. _____

So to hon-or him pa-rum pum pum pum, _ when_ we come. _
Shall I play for you, pa-rum pum pum pum, _ on _my drum?_
Then he smiled at me pa-rum pum pum pum, _ me and my drum. _

Can you be the drummer?
Play these patterns on the drum as you sing.

Verses 1 and 2

pum   pum   pum   pum

Verse 3

pum, rum pum pum, rum pum pum   rum pum pum, rum pum

Can you find a special place to add this sound?

LOVE SOMEBODY

American Folk Song

1. Love some-bod-y, yes I do,
2. Love some-bod-y, can't guess who,

Love some-bod-y, yes I do,
Love some-bod-y, can't guess who,

Love some-bod-y, yes I do,
Love some-bod-y, can't guess who,

Love some-bod-y but I won't tell who.
Love some-bod-y but I won't tell who.

Refrain

Love some-bod-y, yes I do,

Love some-bod-y, yes I do,

150

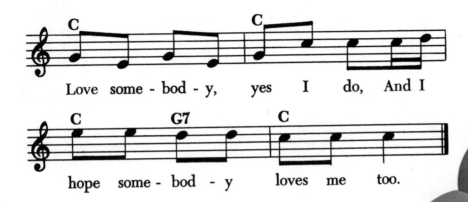

Love some-bod-y, yes I do, And I

hope some-bod-y loves me too.

3. Love somebody's eyes of blue, *(3 times)*
   Love somebody but I won't tell who.
   Refrain
4. Love somebody's smile so true, *(3 times)*
   Love somebody but I won't tell who.
   Refrain

Can you find two large sections in this song?
What helps you know when a new section begins?

GREETING PRELUDE

by Igor Stravinsky

What special time does this music suggest?
Listen. Can you guess the name of the melody?

Did you guess the melody?
What was different about the way it was performed?

AMERICA, THE BEAUTIFUL

Words by Katharine Lee Bates

Music by Samuel A. Ward

CLASSIFIED INDEX

DANCES

Chebogah, 58
Skip to My Lou, 71
Willowbee, 53

FOLK SONGS
FROM OTHER LANDS

Africa
African Noel, 143
Gazelle, The, 40
Ingonyama, 51

Belgium
Donkeys and Carrots, 33

Bohemia
Wondering, 68

Canada
Land of the Silver Birch, 109

China
Spring Song, 81

Denmark
Harvest Song, 139

England
Ah, Poor Bird, 91
Derry Ding Ding Dason, 23

France
Little Prince, The, 57
Sur le Pont d'Avignon, 72
Tell Us Gentlemen, 8

Israel
Al Hasela, 102

Italy
Come Boating With Me, 25

Japan
Cherry Bloom, 106
Hitori de Sabishii, 73

Netherlands
My Aunt Grete, 42
Sarasponda, 32

Polynesia
Tongo, 86

Spain
I've a Fine Bonny Castle, 10

Wales
Deck the Halls, 144

West Indies
Tinga Layo, 49

HOLIDAYS AND SPECIAL TIMES

African Noel, 143
America the Beautiful, 152
Deck the Halls, 144
Little Drummer Boy, The, 148
Love Somebody, 150
Hallowe'en, 137
Hanukah, 142
There are Many Flags in Many Lands, 140
This House Is Haunted, 29
'Twas in the Moon of Wintertime, 146
Unbirthday Song, The, 136

LISTENING LESSONS

Air from *Suite No. 3 in D Major*
    (J. S. Bach), 123
Anitra's Dance from *Peer Gynt Suite*
    (E. Grieg), 15
Banshee (*H. Cowell*), 138

Cattle (*V. Thomson*), 111

Dance of the Comedians (*B. Smetana*), 117

Evolutions (*H. Badings*), 116

Greeting Prelude (*I. Stravinsky*), 151

Hansel and Gretel (*E. Humperdinck*), 64

Hungarian Dance No. 1 in G minor
  (*J. Brahms*), 60

Minuet from *Sinfonia No. 1 in G Major* (*D. Scarlatti*), 11

Moto Perpetuo (*B. Britten*), 55

Music Box Waltz (*D. Shostakovitch*), 116

Pictures at an Exhibition (*M. Moussorgsky*), 36

Pumpkineater's Little Fugue (*R. McBride*), 122

Rondeau (*H. Purcell*), 47

Russian Sailors' Dance from *The Red Poppy* (*R. Glière*), 9

Steel Foundry, The, from *Symphony of Machines* (*A. Mossolov*), 6

Tambourin (*J. P. Rameau*), 20

Three to Get Ready (*D. Brubeck*), 116

Variation on a Korean Folk Song
  (*J. B. Chance*), 127

ROUNDS

Ah, Poor Bird, 91

Canoe Song, 93

Derry Ding Ding Dason, 23

Donkeys and Carrots, 33

For Health and Strength, 129

Row, Row, Row Your Boat, 56

POEMS AND CHANTS

Banshee, The, 138

Between Birthdays, 136

Building a Car, 50

Cherry Blossoms, 107

Crossing, 30

Dream Dust, 118

Gilly's Band, 100

Jungle, The, 125

Little Bird, 107

Mice, 46

Peter Piper, 92

Rain Chant, 108

Snake, The, 80

Sower, The, 46

To the Korner Krinklestein, 85

Whoop-De-Dah! 45

Why, Sir? 17

ALPHABETICAL INDEX

Accompany Songs You Know, 34
African Noel, 143
Ah, Poor Bird, 91
Air from *Suite No. 3 in D Major (J. S. Bach),*
    123
Al Hasela, 102
All the Little Babies, 24
America the Beautiful, 152
Anitra's Dance from *Peer Gynt Suite (E. Grieg),*
    15
Ants Go Marching, The, 44
Artist, The, 126
At a Georgia Camp Meeting, 101
At the Gate of Heaven, 96

Banshee *(H. Cowell),* 138
Banshee, The, 138
Between Birthdays, 136
Building a Car, 50

Canoe Song, 93
Cattle *(V. Thomson),* 111
Chebogah, 58
Cherry Bloom, 106
Cherry Blossoms, 107
Children, 1
Childsong, 98
Cloud Song, 14
Come Boating with Me, 25
Composition for Autoharp, A, 128
Create a Composition, 46
Crossing, 30

Dance of the Comedians *(B. Smetana),* 117
Deck the Halls, 144
Department Store, The: a Drama, 62
Derry Ding Ding Dason, 23
Donkeys and Carrots, 33
Dream Dust, 118
Drums, Drums, Drums, 77

Evolutions *(H. Badings),* 116
Explore Harmony on the Autoharp, 70
Explore the Instruments of the String Family,
    123

For Health and Strength, 129
Form a Special Performing Group, 95
Four in a Boat, 19

Gazelle, The, 40
Get on Board, 74
Gilly's Band, 100
Goat, The, 87

Goodbye, Old Paint, 110
Greeting Prelude *(I. Stravinsky),* 151

Hallowe'en, 137
Hansel and Gretel *(E. Humperdinck),* 64
Hanukah, 142
Harvest Song, 139
Hawaiian Rainbows, 48
Hill and Gully Rider, 112
Hitori de Sabishii, 73
How Do You Measure Up? (1), 21
How Do You Measure Up? (2), 39
How Do You Measure Up? (3), 61
How Do You Measure Up? (4), 81
Hungarian Dance No. 1 in G minor
    (J. Brahms), 60

I Love the Mountains, 76
I'm a Nut, 26
I'm Going Away to See Aunt Dinah, 35
Ingonyama, 51
It's a Small World, 120
I've a Fine Bonny Castle, 10

Jungle, The, 125

Land of the Silver Birch, 109
Let's Build a Town, 4
Let's Go Fly a Kite, 114
Little Bird, 107
Little Drummer Boy, The, 148
Little Prince, The, 57
Lone Star Trail, 22
Long John, 2
Love Somebody, 150

Making Up a Two-Part Song, 80
Melody for Autoharp, A, 129
Mice, 46
Michael, Row the Boat Ashore, 94
Minuet from *Sinfonia No. 1 in G Major*
    (D. Scarlatti), 11
Moto Perpetuo *(B. Britten),* 55
Move Around—Change Around, 3
Music Box Waltz *(D. Shostakovitch),* 116
My Aunt Grete, 42
My Nature Song, 107
My Old Hen, 69

Night Herding Song, 130
Noble Duke of York, The, 27

Old Texas, 31

Perform . . . Alone . . . With Others, 31
Perform . . . Move . . . Speak, 30
Peter Piper, 92
Pictures at an Exhibition *(M. Moussorgsky)*, 36
Pumpkineater's Little Fugue *(R. McBride)*, 122

Rain Chant, 108
Raindrops, 82
Rainstorm, 28
Rondeau *(H. Purcell)*, 47
Row, Row, Row Your Boat, 56
Russian Sailors' Dance, *(R. Glière)*, 9

Sandy Land, 43
Sarasponda, 32
Scales and Arpeggios, 54
Search for Sounds, 124
Siamese Cat Song, The, 12
Skip to My Lou, 71
Snake, The, 80
Sower, The, 46
Spring Song, 81
Steel Foundry, The, *(A. Mossolov)*, 6
Sur le Pont d'Avignon, 72

Tambourin, *(J. P. Rameau)*, 20
Tell Us, Gentlemen, 8

There Are Many Flags in Many Lands, 140
There's a Little Wheel A-Turnin', 79
This House Is Haunted, 29
Three To Get Ready *(D. Brubeck)*, 116
Tinga Layo, 49
Tongo, 86
To the Korner Krinklestein, 85
Trail to Mexico, 88
Turn the Glasses Over, 104
'Twas in the Moon of Wintertime, 146

Ugly Duckling, The, 132
Unbirthday Song, The, 136

Variation on a Korean Folk Song *(J. B. Chance)*, 127

Walk Together, Children, 78
Way Down Yonder in the Brickyard, 52
Whole—Part: a Dance—a Poem, 16
Whoop-De-Dah! 45
Who's That Yonder? 18
Why, Sir? 17
Willowbee, 53
Wondering, 68

You, the Accompanist, 105
You Visit the Art Museum, 38

ILLUSTRATION CREDITS

Color illustrations by Marilyn Bass/Marvin Goldman. Black and white drawings and color line art by Tom Cardamone. Drawing on pages 6–7 by Kevin Credle. Rocket illustration on page 84 by Carl Dickuth. Illustration on page 116 by Bernie Schoenbaum.

Editorial Development Lois Eskin, Alice Trimmer
Editorial Processing Margaret M. Byrne, Regina Chilcoat
Art and Production Frank P. Lamacchia, Vivian Fenster, Fred C. Pusterla, Robin Swenson, Russell Dian, Barbara Orzech, Anita Dickhuth, Iris Kleinman, Ellen Lokiec
Product Manager J. Edward Johnson
Advisory Board James Boyd, William G. Jones, David Joy, Sheila Nettles
Consultants Sheila Nettles, Ruth Spies
Researchers Eileen Kelly, Pamela Floch, Gerard LaVan